DEATH VALLEY

A GUIDE

AMERICAN GUIDE SERIES

DEATH VALLEY

A GUIDE

Written and compiled by the Federal Writers' Project of the Works Progress Administration of Northern California

Updated with the cooperation of the
National Park Service Staff
Death Valley, California

Edited by Cheri Rae

OLYMPUS PRESS
SANTA BARBARA · 1991

Cover design and illustration by Deja Hsu
Photograph courtesy National Park Service.

Book design and typography by Jim Cook

PHOTO CREDITS:
National Park Service: 9, 33, 38, 42 (3), 43, 45, 49, 60, 93, 96, 110, 111, 120, 142, 143; NPS/Charles Addams: 21; NPS/H.F. Cameron: 129; NPS/H.D. Curry: 14, 57, 84, 90 (inset), 91; NPS/Burton Frasher, Sr.: 47, 72, 73; NPS/Richard Frear: 31, 51, 82, 83, 88, 90, 97, 101, 12, 113, 119; NPS/George Grant: 71, 76 89, 105, 108; NPS/Grunigen: 22; NPS/P.G. Sanchez: 40; NPS/E.L. Sumner, Jr.: 58; Cheri Rae, 67; U.S. Borax: 61.

ACKNOWLEDGEMENTS:
The editor wishes to thank the Park Rangers and staff of Death Valley National Monument who assisted in the production of this project. Special thanks to Ed Rothfuss, Park Superintendent; Ross Hopkins, Supervisory Park Ranger; Jim Pisarowicz, Executive Director, Death Valley Natural History Association; Shirley Harding, Park Curator; Dave Heffner, Death Valley '49ers; Jed Tuttle, Museum Technician; Kari Coughlin, Friends of Rhyolite; David Yim, Park Ranger; Karen Duggan, Museum Technician.
Thanks also to UCLA Research Library/Special Collections.

DISCLAIMER:
Although the publisher has made every effort to ensure the information herein was correct at the time of going to press, the publisher does not assume and hereby disclaims any liability to any party for any loss or damage caused by errors, omissions, or any potential travel disruption whether such errors or omissions result from negligence, accident, or any other cause.

LIBRARY OF CONGRESS CATALOGING-IN-PUBLICATION DATA
Death Valley: the 1938 WPA guide / written and compiled by the Federal
  Writers' Project of the Works Progress Administration of Northern
  California; Foreword by Cheri Rae; Introduction by Park Superintendent
  Ed Rothfuss. —Updated for today's traveler.
    p.   cm.
  Originally published: Boston: Houghton Mifflin, 1939, in series: American
guide series.
  Includes bibliographical references and index.
  ISBN 0-934161-10-0: $10.95
    1. Death Valley (Calif. and Nev.)—Description and travel—Guide books.
  I. Federal Writers' Project of the Works Progress Administration of Northern
  California.
  F868.D2D436   1991   91-26286
  917.94'870453—dc20   CIP

Table of Contents

A map of Death Valley appears on pages 24–25

FOREWORD

Death Valley: The 1938 WPA Guide Updated for Today's Traveler

Originally titled *Death Valley: A Guide,* this volume was written in 1938 as part of the American Guide Series produced by the Federal Writers' Project. To defray costs to the government, the book was sponsored by the Bret Harte Associates, a nonprofit organization founded by San Francisco novelist Charles Caldwell Dobie. Published in 1939 by Houghton Mifflin, it sold for one dollar.

Although Project writers generally were uncredited, staff member Cora Vernon Lee is mentioned in the original foreword as the primary writer and the person with the vision and energy behind this book. Although Lee's interest in the subject is obvious from her work, it's difficult for today's researcher to discover anything about her.

Imagine a spunky woman, leaving the Project office in San Francisco for the wide-open—and almost uncharted—spaces of Death Valley. Lee insisted on working in the heat of the summer for the most authentic experience possible.

The book's purpose was twofold: to tell the story of Death Valley and to function as an on-site guidebook to enable visitors to explore the place. It succeeded on both counts, and does so today as well.

Because the book was carefully researched and meticulously fact-checked by a host of writers and editors, the nature and history notes hold up well, as do descriptions of landforms and viewpoints. But it's the quality of the writing—clear, concise and full of interesting quotes and anecdotes from old-timers—that gives the book its timeless appeal. Most travel writing of the 1930s, especially works about the desert, are characterized by boosterism and hyperbole that obscure the essence of a place; not so in this guide.

In short, the book is a very good guide to what Death Valley was like many years ago. It's a chance to glimpse Death Valley as it was when first designated a National Monument and made accessible to the general public.

The traveler who picks up the WPA guide to Los Angeles, Santa Barbara or Monterey will have some difficulty using the book as a guide, since those areas have been substantially transformed. This Death Valley guide, however, is still surprisingly accurate. It details then-populated mining towns and Indian camps; with a few exceptions, most of the land features described are very much the same as they were more than 50 years ago.

Elevations may have been exaggerated a bit, or just measured inaccurately, and prices have changed considerably. Some of the places are now gone, washed away, reduced to rubble over time—Gnomes' Workshop, the Indian Trading Post, Chris Wicht's Camp, the monorail in Wingate Pass—and a few suggested tours are now within the nearby Naval Weapons Center, but the information presented here reads like a moment frozen in time.

The 1930s

While many readers may be familiar with America during the 1930s— from first-hand knowledge or reading historical accounts—a short explanation may be in order. The darkest days of the Great Depression hit every class, every occupation. Plumbers and poets, waitresses and writers, bankers and railroad workers—all suffered anxiety over impending poverty and worse. Some ended up on breadlines; many lost not only their livelihoods, but their homes and families, their hopes and dreams.

"Hoovervilles," camps of homeless people, sprung up on the outskirts of many cities; hunger became a reality in what had always been the land of plenty. When fully one-third of the workforce was unemployed, a sense of hopelessness settled on the populace.

At least some relief began when President Franklin Roosevelt initiated the New Deal, a series of bold Federal programs designed to promote economic recovery and improve social conditions. While many New Deal programs had wide-ranging effects throughout the nation, two of them—the Civilian Conservation Corps (CCC) and the Works Projects Administration (WPA) were to have great impact on the development of Death Valley.

The CCC

The CCC operated for just nine years; during that time it employed some three million workers who fanned out across America in 4,500 camps. They built facilities in 800 state and national parks, nearly 50,000 bridges, about 4,000 historic structures and 5,000 miles of water lines. The men planted 45 million trees in park areas, and nearly three billion seedlings in reforestation and erosion prevention projects.

Life with the CCC was rough and rigorous. Crewmembers lived in tent camps and barracks; they performed back-breaking physical labor

Mesquite Springs: CCC Spike Camp, 1934

for which they were paid $25 a month. Under terms of the CCC contract, $20 was sent directly to the crewmember's family, while he received just $5 a month to cover his expenses.

It was honest work for discouraged, unemployed men who really had few other options. They joined from rural areas of the South, the cities of the Northeast, and throughout the West and Midwest. Many of them were young, relatively unskilled laborers who took advantage of the government-sponsored program in order to assist their families and learn a trade.

In October 1933, just seven months after the designation of Death Valley as a National Monument, two CCC companies were assigned to the area, joined by several additional companies in the following years.

Somehow coping with the stresses of performing hard labor in an alien land under the harshest conditions, CCC workers managed to turn Death Valley into an accessible destination. During just their first three years in Death Valley, CCC crews built 343 miles of new roads, developed a dozen springs and wells; they constructed several campgrounds and picnic facilities, three ranger stations and the Park Village residences. Much of their work is still intact today, including the Furnace Creek concessions complex.

While the buildings exhibit that "period" feel common to those constructed in the 1930s (and seen in many National Park Service facilities built by CCC companies across the nation), it's the engineering of roads that really stands out as one of the major accomplishments of the CCC in Death Valley.

The roadwork provides access to Death Valley and many of its more remote areas while complementing the natural features of the land. The road engineers and crewmen heeded the cautionary notes of NPS Superintendent John B. White when he wrote to Director Albright in 1931:

> One thought from a landscape point of view occurs to me, and that is that Death Valley may need protection from road builders. Good, high, grade approach roads are needed from both sides, but it would be a landscape crime to put a paved road, or several paved roads over the floor of Death Valley where there are now meandering desert roads. Any scheme of development should include careful landscaping of the roads.

10

We can be thankful to this day that no such "landscape crime" occurred. The driver in a hurry may complain, but there are still no paved roads destroying the broad valley floor.

The CCC was disbanded in 1942, when America entered World War II. The workers have been called "the heroes of Death Valley" and "the answer to the National Park Service prayer." Indeed, it's doubtful that the infrastructure of Death Valley could have been created so quickly, or so well if not for the timely creation of that sizable low-paid Federal work force. Thanks to the CCC, visitors ever since have been able to safely venture into the remote area.

The WPA

In February 1935, desperate writers had taken to the streets, demanding some sort of government assistance. "Children Need Books. Writers Need A Break. We Demand Projects," read the sign of one picketer. By spring, Congress passed the Emergency Relief Act of 1935, and FDR signed an Executive Order creating the WPA.

The WPA was a bold, innovative concept designed to put unemployed creative types—writers, actors, artists amd musicians—back to work. Several arts projects fell under the supervision of the Works Projects Administration, including the Federal Writers' Project.

The project served as a lifeline for the writing community which was particularly hard-hit during the Depression. Magazines virtually stopped buying articles; royalty payments nearly dried up and few new contracts were commissioned. Yet the writers still had families to support, rent to pay, other living expenses to meet.

On their applications for employment, many writers revealed their desperation. One pleaded for a job noting, "The wolf is at my door." Another completed the questions:

> *Kind of work:* Will accept any position
> *Salary:* Enough to make a living on
> *At present:* Broke.

One of the primary tasks of the Federal Writers' Project was to create a series of guidebooks entitled the American Guide Series. The books were the first written by and for Americans specifically intended to define and describe the land, people and culture of America. Director of the Federal Writers' Project Henry Alsberg described the task: "A genuine, valuable and objective contribution to the understanding of American life."

After much debate among administrators, the guidebook format was reached—a compromise between chamber of commerce-type boosterism and encyclopedia-like listings of information. Each of the books in this American Guide Series featured essays on the land, its history and cultural characteristics, along with meticulously researched driving tours.

Never before had a nation attempted to subsidize the production of literature—or any arts projects—at such a level. At its height in 1936, the Project employed more than 6,500 writers, editors, proofreaders, and fact-checkers.

Although the official policy of the Project was to insist on anonymity, several writers who worked for the Project later emerged as among the most significant voices of contemporary America—Saul Bellow, Richard Wright, Ralph Ellison, John Cheever, Loren Eiseley, Conrad Aiken and Kenneth Rexroth.

It seems no one was ever totally pleased with the Project. Many writers considered the writing of guidebooks beneath them; most became frustrated with administrative efforts to quantify their productivity and amount of time they were required to spend on the projects. Guidebook writing left little time or energy for more creative pursuits.

One revealed his resentment when he wrote, "A tour is a tour is a tour . . . a main tour, side tour, well-paved tour, graveled tour. . . ." Another penned the "Psalm of Touring":

> Tell me not in mournful numbers
> That a tour is but a dream
> That the highway never blunders
> And maps are just what they seem.

Despite overwhelmingly positive critical reviews of the work produced, the public perceived the Project as an expensive and wasteful use of their tax dollars. By 1939, the WPA was increasingly under fire. Headlines screamed "Nation Described at $1 a Word." Some critics speculated that the initials WPA stood for "We Poke Along." The nation's press published charges of incompetence at high levels and disputed the political and cultural content of the guides.

Finally, Congress got into the act with the Committee to Investigate Un-American Activities. The Project was termed a "red nest" that published "insidious propaganda" and promoted "class hatred."

As a result, loyalty oaths were demanded of workers. Federal funding was slashed; it finally ceased in the spring of 1939. (State and local funding allowed some projects to continue, but many more were completed, but never published.) When America entered World War II, the WPA turned to war themes: pamphlets detailed civil defense procedures, how to plant a home victory garden, and accounts of military history. Even state and local funding ended in 1942.

Although several in-progress projects were halted before publication, in just over seven years, the Project produced more than a thousand publications, including full-length books, pamphlets and booklets—at a cost of $27 million.

That so much more is known about Death Valley CCC workers than their WPA counterparts is probably not surprising. It has to do with the nature of work. Unlike grading roads, digging wells and constructing buildings, the work of writing hardly seems like work to those who don't do it themselves. While CCC workers have been hailed as heroes, WPA workers labored in obscurity.

FDR's vision of the experimental Project had been to create a "literature of nationhood." The American Guide Series has been called the "biggest, fastest, most original research job in the history of the world." In his American travelog, *Travels With Charley*, John Steinbeck notes, "The complete set comprises the most comprehensive account of the United States ever got together."

Touring Death Valley

While U.S. Borax and a few individuals did a little to promote tourism in Death Valley in the 1920s, it wasn't until the 1930s—and the establishment of Death Valley National Monument—that visitors flocked to the area.

It was a time when the public's perception of the desert was changing. Land that had once feared for its harshness was suddenly

Cooling off in Furnace Creek Inn, 1939

celebrated for its unique beauty. Popular literature—ranging from local newspapers to a series in *The Saturday Evening Post*—was full of breathless accounts of the scenic splendor of Death Valley; one of the most popular radio shows of the 1930s was "Death Valley Days." (The radio show eventually evolved into a long-running television show hosted by then-actor Ronald Reagan.)

America was in love with the desert. Railroads and touring companies were in place, auto touring was heavily promoted, and even a few hotels offered comfort to plucky travelers who wanted to investigate Death Valley for themselves. Everything looked rosy for big tourism business until the Great Depression took hold of the economy.

In a sense, though, the Depression was a great stroke of luck for Death Valley. It was the efforts of the CCC and WPA workers that created access to the new national monument. They worked at a time when comparatively few Americans were traveling. When post-war adventurers hit the road again, they discovered a nearly brand-new national monument full of intriguing sights.

Actually, travel to Death Valley did not cease entirely during the Depression. In 1933, the newly named National Monument received

9,000 visitors; by 1939, the number increased to nearly 60,000. By 1976, Death Valley was attracting 600,000 visitors yearly; today more than 800,000.

Today's visitors to Death Valley flock from all over the world, all year-round. During the winter months, much of the visitation is by retired "snowbirds" camping in their motorhomes or trailers. But during the summer months, you're more likely to hear visitors speaking German, French, Japanese.

They find facilities unimagined by the unfortunate Manly party that stumbled into the bare land so many years ago. They drive in air-conditioned comfort, stay in comfortable hotel rooms or well-maintained campgrounds, order meals and purchase provisions at concessions in the park, even quaff a beer or two at the local saloon. They may browse through museums; take a swim in an Olympic-size pool; tour a Moorish castle; shop for souvenirs; enjoy the desert landscape while hiking along an interpretive path, referring to the brochure purchased at the kiosk located at the side of the road.

Death Valley is currently administered as a National Monument by the National Park Service. Thanks to the efforts of hard-working environmentalists and members of Congress, Death Valley may soon receive the highest accolade of a unit in America's National Park System—designation as a National Park.

CHERI RAE
Editor

Santa Barbara, California
1991

INTRODUCTION

A few of my lifelong loves have been exploring America's National Parks, and reading and collecting books. In the past decade, reading books about parks and history, the natural and physical sciences has become a serious hobby.

My own introduction to old and out-of-print books began seriously when, as a geology student, I searched the shelves of a used-book store for inexpensive textbooks. There, in a dark corner in a dusty shop on High Street in Columbus, Ohio, I discovered two small volumes that are a prized part of my library today. One is Marshall B. Gardner's 1913 edition, *A Journal to the Earth's Interior*—Gardner really believed he had sailed into the earth's interior via the North Pole, the Earth's "iris"! The second is an 1886 guidebook by E.I. Massy, *The Tarawera Eruption;* its margins are filled with intriguing annotations penned by the long-ago tourist who used this book during a visit to New Zealand about the turn of the century.

These books awakened my curiousity to explore the hidden treasures to be found in old volumes, and stimulated my lifelong interest—some say passion—for old books.

A couple of years ago, I was excited to find a copy of *Death Valley*, part of the American Guide Series, in the original dust jacket. What a find! The book was—and is—well written, containing wonderful details about Death Valley. Although written more than 50 years ago, most of it (except the prices and a few features) is as fresh and valid today.

It was through these pages that I rediscovered little bits of Death Valley history that were lost over time and the result of the inevitable turnover of park employees. Here I first learned that in 1938 the Park Service had a nursery at Cow Creek, where employees raised desert holly and mesquite to help restore native plants in the Valley. (Today, three employee residences are located on the site.)

It was in this fascinating text, and the accompanying map, that I first learned of the Gnomes' Workshop. This delightful area was taken off the maps after a flash flood removed many of the two- to three-feet high "gnomes." Using the guide, we relocated this area, and found that time is slowly healing nature's ravages. Today, the alkaline formations are growing, and many are several feet high. It's once again a delightful short hike, and we often take friends there.

Although Death Valley was first brought to the attention of the American public in another classic, John R. Spear's 1892 *Illustrated Sketches of Death Valley*, it was not seriously considered a potential national park until the mid-1920s.

The National Park Service was established by an act of Congress on August 25, 1916, with the following declaration:

> The Service thus established shall promote and regulate the use of the Federal areas known as National Parks, monuments and reservations hereinafter specifically by such means and measures which conform to the fundamental purpose of the said parks, monuments and reservations, which purpose is to conserve the scenery and the natural and historic objects and the wildlife therein, and to provide for the enjoyment of the same in such manner and by such means as will leave them unimpaired for the enjoyment of future generations.

Because the challenges to our parks are greater today, this mandate is even more important than when drafted more than 75 years ago. Today, Death Valley faces the potential of urban growth in the arid Southwest, along with its impact on the water supply and air quality. We continually need to defend our parks.

Eleven years after the establishment of the National Park Service, the Pacific Coast Borax Company invited the Service's director, Stephen T. Mather, and his field service director, Horace M. Albright (Inyo County native and soon to be the NPS's second director), to visit Death Valley. The two stayed at the new tourist facility, the Furnace Creek Inn, in January 1927, just one month before it opened. Mather and Albright, although no strangers to Death Valley, were impressed with the potential of making the area a national park (which of course, was the motive and proposal of the Borax people).

I recall Albright telling me a few years ago (he died in 1987 at the age of 97) that the reason they did not press for park status was the combination of active mining (not compatible with the policy of the NPS), and the appearance of conflict of interests. Mather had formerly worked for the Borax Company (the 20 Mule Team slogan was his idea), and both he and Albright were Californians. At the time, California already had more national parks than any other state (four of the 19 designated up to that time) and there was a move afoot to add Redwoods.

Albright later was named director of the National Park Service. Before leaving office, he prepared the February 11, 1933, proclamation that established Death Valley as a national monument. He never lost his interest in and love of Death Valley. Upon my accepting the appointment to the superintendency of Death Valley in August 1982, I had the privilege to meet and get to know him.

Over the years, I received a dozen or more letters from Albright— all painfully typed, as he said, "by my 1890 fingers on my 1932 typewriter," and evidenced by the erratic spacing and carefully inked corrections. Each letter contained questions about visitation, and the status of mining. He offered advice about how to deal with "so and so," offered assistance in making contacts and provided letters of introduction. He was proud of Death Valley and wanted to see things go well—and he wanted to see the naming of Death Valley National Park.

Someday Albright's dream will be realized. Death Valley has such diversity, such richness of beauty: its colors and moods, shapes and patterns; landforms ranging from rugged mountains to the salt playa; lifeforms ranging from bighorn sheep to desert pupfish, plants that struggle to survive. In its cultural aspects, too, Death Valley is exceptional: the presence of man ranging from Native Americans to miners, the wonders of Scotty's Castle and the curiosity of early tourists.

With this richness in heritage, Death Valley truly occupies a special place in the National Park system, and among world-class parks—one that commands our respect, our love, our appreciation, our support.

During the past 33 years, I've been privileged to live and work in nine great national park areas, and have visited more than 100 others. I've often been asked to name my favorite park. Although my standard answer ("The one I'm in now.") has generally been true, I can say with all honesty that Death Valley is, has been, and continues to be my favorite. My nine years as the park superintendent in Death Valley have been the most challenging—not only for the size and diversity of resources, but because of the challenges facing the area.

Death Valley is a special place and it well-deserves this guidebook. Again and again through the pages of this wonderful book, one rediscovers little gems of Death Valley fact and lore. I am elated that Olympus Press chose to reprint this classic, especially because it's during the year that we recognize the seventy-fifth Anniversary of the National Park System.

This classic guidebook gives you a chance to expand your horizons in a truly great National Park!

EDWIN L. ROTHFUSS
Park Superintendent

Death Valley National Monument
1991

Touring Death Valley

How to Use This Book

To maintain the integrity of the original work, we've chosen to let it stand intact, updated at the beginning of each tour with notes about road conditions, historical corrections and information that might enhance your understanding of the place or incident described. A few updated editor's notes appear in the introductory sections of the original text.

Before venturing into any backcountry area, check first with Death Valley park rangers for information about road conditions, safety concerns and travel advisability.

Private Property Remember that the book was written more than 50 years ago; laws regarding land use and private property have changed in some areas. There are several privately owned areas: respect and obey all posted signs, especially in areas where mining claims are in effect.

Natural and Cultural Resources Attitudes about the preservation of desert artifacts have changed significantly since the 1930s. Today, state and federal laws protect all flora, fauna, cultural sites and artifacts including petroglyphs, pictographs and the like. Enjoy the view, take photographs, and leave all such natural and cultural resources undisturbed. Remember that driving off designated roads is expressly prohibited.

Road Conditions Know that road conditions can change dramatically as a result of flash flooding, high winds or other severe weather

For your own safety, check with park rangers before venturing into unfamiliar territory.

Other Notes

❖ Many, but not all, the photographs contained in this volume were published in the first edition. The book design and layout have been substantially updated to fit today's tastes.

❖ Maps contained in this volume are from the original book; except where indicated in the update sections, they have changed very little.

❖ Check with your travel agent for the most complete and up-to-date information about commercial tours to Death Valley. During the season (October through May) the Fred Harvey Company operates tours within the National Monument.

❖ Prices quoted in the text refer to 1938; alas, they have changed dramatically since then.

For Your Own Good

"Death" Valley is no joke; it's a harsh environment, a place that must be met on its own terms. Visitors must adapt to harsh conditions unlike those encountered anywhere else.

There have been all too many cases when individuals have overestimated their own fitness, underestimated the rigors of desert travel. Be smart, cautious and careful when venturing into any desert land. Use common sense, make sure your vehicle is in good repair, and heed all Death Valley park warnings, safety tips and regulations.

Park Regulations

❖ Camp only in designated sites; roadside camping is prohibited.

❖ Collecting, gathering, cutting, or disturbing plants, rocks, or any natural or historic feature is not allowed.

❖ Please dispose of trash in the receptacles provided and place a bucket under your sink drain.

❖ Do not drive off established roads.

❖ Pets must be leashed at all times. They are not allowed in the Visitor Center or other public buildings, or in the backcountry.

❖ This is a wildlife sanctuary. Carrying firearms that are not cased or otherwise rendered inoperative is prohibited.

❖ Shooting firearms, even at targets, is not allowed.

Safety

❖ Do not enter mine shafts, tunnels or old buildings.

❖ Watch for rattlesnakes, especially near old structures or vegetated areas near water.

❖ Be alert for flash floods when it looks stormy.

❖ All animals in the park are wild. They often carry diseases, and they can bite. Do not feed or disturb them.

❖ Always tell someone where you are going and when you expect to return.

❖ Please be sure that your car is in good mechanical condition and that your fuel tank is full before you begin each day's tour. Within the park, gasoline is sold only at Furnace Creek, Scotty's Castle, and Stovepipe Wells.

❖ Park roads are designed for your enjoyment of the scenery, not for speed. Please observe posted speed limits, and wear your seat belt.

Furnace Creek Wash: flood damage, August 2, 1942.

❖ Be aware that hot weather hiking can be risky. Carry at least one gallon of water per person per day of hiking.

❖ Make your visit to Death Valley a safe, enjoyable one!

Campgrounds

❖ Death Valley National Monument operates nine campgrounds throughout the monument, with a total of 1500 campsites. Expect periods of heavy use from October through April, especially during the Death Valley '49ers Encampment during early November.

Warm Weather Hints

Take Care of Yourself

❖ Stay away from the salt flats in hot weather. Ground temperatures can exceed 200 degrees, and distances are deceiving in the clear, dry air.

❖ Thirst is a warning of your body's need for water. Carry plenty of water—one gallon per day—and drink it freely, every hour or so.

❖ Salt is not a substitute for water; ingesting it will not reduce your perspiration rate.

❖ Clothing protects from the sun. Wear a shirt, sunglasses, sturdy shoes and a broad-brimmed hat.

❖ Wind speeds up your evaporation rate; avoid it.

❖ Always hike with at least one other person.

Take Care of Your Car

❖ Watch the temperature of your car motor. Do not "lug" the motor on grades; shift to a lower gear instead.

❖ If the car starts to heat, turn off the air conditioner.

❖ To cool the motor: Turn into the breeze; don't stop the motor; while it is running at a fast idle speed, slowly pour sufficient water over the radiator core to cool it. Cover the radiator cap when removing it to protect yourself from the heat. Slowly fill the radiator to the proper level and proceed.

❖ Do not deflate tires.

❖ Check gasoline and oil before every journey. Services are available only at Stovepipe Wells, Furnace Creek Ranch and Scotty's Castle.

❖ If trouble develops, stay with your car on paved roads.

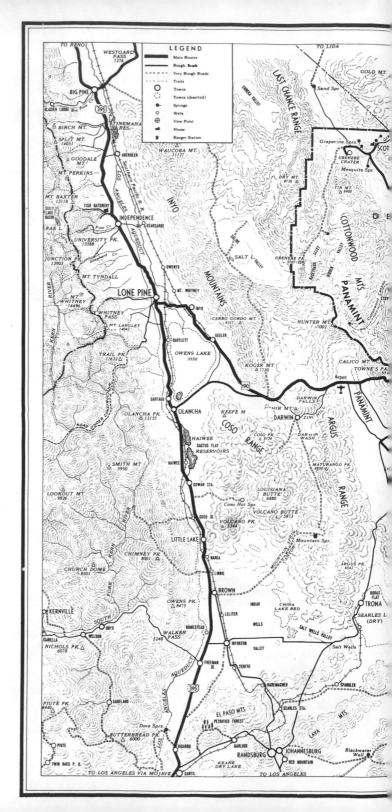

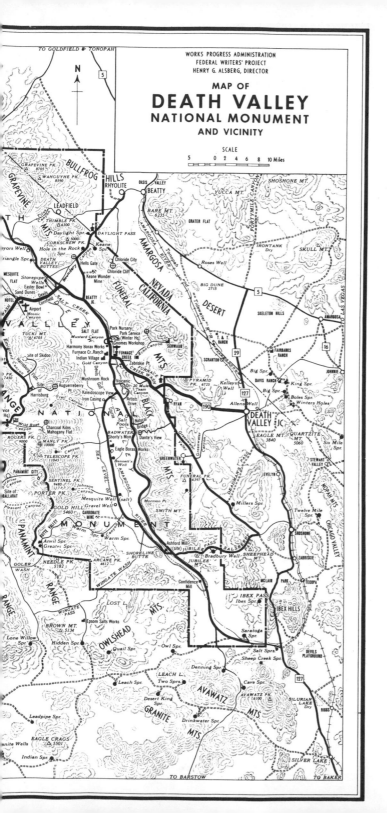

WORKS PROGRESS ADMINISTRATION
FEDERAL WRITERS' PROJECT
HENRY G. ALSBERG, DIRECTOR

MAP OF

DEATH VALLEY
NATIONAL MONUMENT
AND VICINITY

SCALE

5 0 2 4 6 8 10 Miles

General Information

[Ed. Note: Information below circa 1938; see Appendix for updated information.]

Season: October to May; a few main roads open all year.

Climate: Fall and spring, days warm to hot, nights cool. Winter, days cool, nights chilly to cold. Summer extremely hot, days 110° to 130°, nights 80° to 100°; low humidity at all times.

Administrative Offices: National Park Service Headquarters, Death Valley, California.

Admission: No fee; registration of license number of automobile, name and address of owner, number of passengers, required.

Transportation to and in Death Valley *(rates 1938)*

From east or west, Union Pacific Railroad at Crucero, California, connecting with Tonopah and Tidewater Railroad to Death Valley Junction (see Tour 1). Automobile to Death Valley, approximate fare, $5. Tanner Tours pick up Union Pacific Railroad passengers at Las Vegas, Nevada, and Barstow, California; Santa Fe Railway passengers also at Barstow.

Tanner Tours: All-expense by motor from Los Angeles to Death Valley and return, 800-mile trip, 200 miles within Death Valley; 2 passengers minimum, approximately $64.50 per person.

Airfields: Death Valley Airport, opposite Furnace Creek Ranch. Emergency landing fields near Stove Pipe Wells Hotel and in Panamint Valley (unsafe when wet).

On call, airplane service between Death Valley and Las Vegas, Boulder Dam, Boulder Dam Tours, Inc.

Private Guide Service (approximately $2 an hour) and private motor tours (approximately $4 an hour) available at Furnace Creek Camp and Furnace Creek Inn.

More than 300 miles of roads in Monument, 190 miles with oiled surface.

Highway Approaches to Death Valley *(see map)*

From east on Calif. 190, branching from Calif. 127 (at Death Valley Junction); from east on unnumbered road branching from Calif. 127 (N of Shoshone) through Salsberry and Jubilee Passes.

From east, Nevada, on rough unnumbered road branching from Nev. 5 (N. of Beatty) through Grapevine Canyon; on the road from Nev. 5 (at Beatty) through Daylight Pass.

From west on Calif. 190, branching from US 395 (S. of Lone Pine). From south on rough unnumbered road branching from US 466 (E. of Barstow) by Cave and Denning Springs; on unnumbered road branching from US 395 (N. of Mojave) through Wildrose Canyon. Driving time from Los Angeles over these roads is from 7 to 10 hours; from San Francisco, 18 to 24 hours; from Las Vegas, Nevada, 4 hours.

Accommodations

In Death Valley: Furnace Creek Camp, sleeping and housekeeping cabins, restaurant, store; rates begin at $2 a day. Furnace Creek Inn (open Nov. 1–May 1), American Plan; $9.75 a day single, $15 a day double. Stove Pipe Wells Hotel (open Nov. 20–May 1), European plan; $3 a day up. Also sleeping cabins, rates from $1.50 a day, restaurant, coffee shop.

Texas Springs Public Camp: Camp sites, water toilets.

Death Valley Junction: Amargosa Hotel, European plan; dining room, fountain service, garage.

Lone Pine: Hotels, restaurant, store.

Ryan: Death Valley View Hotel.

Wildrose Canyon: Wildrose Station, restaurant, store, service station.

Service Stations

At all resorts. Emergency accommodations and service station in summer at Stove Pipe Wells Hotel and Furnace Creek Camp.

Warnings

Speed limit, 45 miles per hour. Advisable to carry drinking and radiator water. Service stations far apart in many sections. Keep oil and gas checked, and carry additional supplies if itinerary does not include service stations.

Do not travel closed roads without obtaining full information from rangers or from National Park Service Headquarters.

Special Summer Warnings:

Do not attempt to walk in the Valley during the summer. Carry abundant water for passengers and car. Register at the ranger stations at entrances and travel only on roads kept open by the National Park Service, as these are patrolled daily. In case of breakdown, sit quietly in the car and wait until a ranger passes, or until night lessens the heat, when it will be safer to walk for help if near Furnace Creek Camp, Stove Pipe Wells Hotel, or the ranger stations on Emigrant Wash and in Wildrose Canyon. If the distance to these is too great, it is better to wait until the next day for a ranger patrol or other traveler.

Clothing

Both cool and warm clothing advisable in spring and fall; warm clothing for winter; stout shoes for walking.

Equipment

Field glasses desirable. Campers must bring fuel supply; no wood available. Warm bedding needed in winter.

Medical Service

Doctor at Furnace Creek Inn 2 days weekly. Hospitals at Lone Pine and Death Valley Junction. In emergency consult National Park Service Headquarters.

Special Regulations

Disturbance, destruction, defilement, or injury of any ruins, relics, buildings, signs, or other property is prohibited.

Camps, made at designated localities, must be kept clean. Place garbage and tin cans in receptacles provided for that purpose. Use gasoline or kerosene camp stoves, or your own wood.

Death Valley

Ever since the first immigrants saw Death Valley, fantastic tales have been told of its blasting temperatures and stupendous riches, but exaggeration is inevitable in describing this narrow valley of strange, exciting beauty, cradled between towering varicolored mountains. Indians, immigrants, prospectors, miners—all have paused here and left traces; but the Valley, formed by mighty earth movements and sculptured by wind and water, retains a sublime impersonality that has changed little in a million years.

Death Valley

Death Valley, part of the Great American Desert, is largely in southeastern California. In 1933 Death Valley National Monument was established to preserve the area; it now includes a small section in Nevada. The Monument contains 2981 square miles, 500 of which are below sea level. Prior to 1933, Death Valley was largely cared for by the Pacific Coast Borax Company which still conducts the hotels, camps, service stations, and other facilities at Death Valley Junction and Furnace Creek Inn.

The 140-mile curved trough of the Valley lies between steep mountain walls of naked rock, barbaric in coloring. Because it is only six to fifteen miles wide, the vivid rock mountains always rim the horizon. In winter they rear up from the narrow floor in somber splendor; in summer they shimmer in the heat haze that rises from the white pit at their feet. At times their varied hues have the transparent brilliance of incandescent metal—reds, blues, greens, brown, lilacs, purples—and tans, pinks, and grays are splashed and streaked along their sides. This flamboyant coloring does not disturb the great peace and serenity that are the special qualities of Death Valley. The desert quiet is scarcely broken by small, whispering winds and by occasional bird notes. The sky is usually a clear, light blue, but when it is clouded the sunsets are unbelievably gorgeous. At night stars, large in the black velvet sky, roll slowly toward the west.

At one time this valley was occupied by a large lake, long since evaporated, whose ancient shores are indicated by faint benches or terraces on the sides of the Valley. Salts, washed from the mountains in the course of thousands of years, whiten large stretches. The yellow sand dunes and the dry mud flats (*playas*) have the same light tone. Gray gravel fans pour out from canyon mouths to sweep down hundreds of feet to the floor. These fans, looking as smooth as velvet from a distance, are actually channeled by watercourses and studded with great boulders.

Death Valley is divided into two shallow basins by a range of low hills. In the southern basin are the great shimmering Salt Beds; here is the lowest spot in North America, Badwater, 279.6 feet below sea level—only eighty miles away from the highest point in any of the 48 States, Mount Whitney, which rises 14,495 feet above the sea. Both Mount Whitney and Badwater are seen from Dante's View in the

Black Mountains. Death Valley's only river, the Amargosa (Sp.: *bitter one*), in the extreme southern end of the same basin, is a small stream that flows south in Nevada and circles the end of the Black Mountains to flow north and lose itself in the sand and salt. Its water is deeply impregnated with bitter Glauber's and Epsom salts, as are also many springs in the region. The northern basin, smaller than the southern, holds the great tawny Sand Dunes, the white clay beds, and Mesquite Flat.

The Panamint Range, rising 6000 to 11,000 feet above sea level, gives Death Valley its western wall; and the Grapevine, the Funeral, and the Black Mountains, rising 4000 to 8000 feet, form its eastern wall. The Last Chance Range pinches out the northern end of the Valley, and the Avawatz and the Owlshead Mountains block it at the south. Heavy rains occasionally fall on these mountains, run swiftly off the steep slopes, and cascade into the Valley, soon to evaporate. Snow lies lightly on the eastern range, but Telescope Peak in the Panamints is white as late as May. Although Death Valley has the driest climate in North America, it is one of the better-watered deserts because of the many springs in the mountains around it and because of its water-holding marshes.

Telescope Peak

Panamint Valley, just west of Death Valley, is similar in shape though smaller and higher, with an altitude of 1000 to 2000 feet. It is bordered by the Panamint Range on the east, and by the Argus and the Slate Ranges on the west. The southern end is very narrow; great heaps of sand dunes are in the extreme northern end, and in the middle are mud playas, salt beds, and low rubble hills.

Just east of Death Valley is the Amargosa Desert. This desert is 3850 feet high at its northern end and slopes to 2000 feet at a point south of Death Valley Junction. The ghost town of Rhyolite is on the eastern edge of this plateau, at the edge of the Bullfrog Hills.

Scattered through the area are the ghosts of short-lived mining towns; a few walls, weathered boards, and bottles are all that mark many of the sites. But there are still mines in the Panamints, many of them owned and worked by men who knew the feverish days of Rhyolite, Skidoo, Ballarat, and Darwin. These men are brown and lean—for desert heat does not encourage accumulation of fat; and they are friendly to those who love their barren, mysterious desert.

In a world of constant change, where cities rise swiftly in wild places, where green forests turn overnight to ash heaps or black scars, where fertile prairies become shifting dust, Death Valley changes little from decade to decade; its desert plants seem no fewer, no more, and little vagrant winds contine to carry the same faint, dry odor of earth and rock, and to sing the same soft, tuneless songs. Everything in the Valley seems constant but color; it varies with the changing light, ranging through an infinite variety of tones, from the bleached, exhausted ones seen under the blazing summer sun to the rich hues that glow in splendor under the low gray sky of a winter day.

Geology

Almost the whole record of known geological time is seen in the Death Valley region, for it contains rocks of all the great divisions: Archean, Algonkian, Paleozoic, Mesozoic, and Cenozoic. But frequent and profound earth movements have so folded, faulted, and tilted the strata that the story is difficult to read. During the Mesozoic era this was probably a region of low mountains and wide valleys with streams and lakes. During this period there were many earthquakes, and much

volcanic action, with flows of volcanic mud and lava and with frag-
mental material accumulating and forming tuffs. It was in this era,
also, that Death Valley was created by faulting. As can be seen, the
strata of the Panamint and the Black Mountains tilt in the same
direction; the Panamints dip at a long angle toward Death Valley, with
a steeper face toward Panamint Valley, while the Black Mountains
present an abrupt face to the Valley and slope gently eastward toward
the Amargosa Desert. For a long time Death Valley was a desert. Then
it was filled with a lake, which gradually evaporated, and the land
again became a desert. In the last few thousands of years, almost no
changes have taken place, except erosion of the mountains, the
accumulation of the debris in the Valley, and the formation of the
Ubehebe Crater.

Climate

During the fall and spring months Death Valley is delightful, with
warm, sunny days. December and January are the coolest months, but
the days are warm when the sun shines, which is much of the time;
and though the nights are cold, the thermometer seldom drops to
freezing. Only once has a recorded winter temperature been as low as
15°.

In May the sun becomes fiercer, and from the middle of June to the
middle of September it pours concentrated heat into the white valley.
Through July and August the high of the day is usually between 120°
and 128°. A temperature of 134° was once recorded at Furnace Creek
Ranch in a louvered box. (This is only 2° below the world's record
temperature, measured in Morocco.) [Ed. Note: The highest temperature ever recorded was actually 136° in Libya in 1936.] The nights of
this period are also hot, the temperature rarely falling below 85°. In
the summer of 1937, when the recorded temperature was 116°, a
thermometer was laid on the ground while a grave was being dug for a
man who had died in one of the canyons and been carried out by his
companions. When this thermometer registered 156°, it was feared
that it might break, and it was moved into the shade. These high
temperatures, however, are not at all comparable with like temperatures in humid areas.

Those descending into Death Valley in July and August meet intense heat at an altitude of 1500 feet. The breeze engendered by the movement of a car is cooling, though the car's metal trimmings become hot enough to burn the skin of a person so foolish as to come into contact with them. Experienced people, who live in the Monument during the summer, can estimate temperature within a few degrees by holding a hand out of the car, back upward; they base their estimates on the length of time it takes the sunlight to cause a sharp pain at the base of the nails.

As a rule the heat slows down mental processes, making it more difficult to cope with emergencies. The air is so dry that perspiration dries almost as soon as it forms, and it leaves a coating of salt, as gritty as fine sand, on the skin. The skin is flushed as the blood races close to the surface to take advantage of the cooling caused by the evaporation of perspiration.

Such heat is not to be trifled with, as the various graves in Death Valley attest, but it is not unendurable; some people stay here all summer. At the Park Nursery, just above sea level, a good supply of water keeps the grass growing throughout the summer, though it becomes dry and rusty. At Furnace Creek Ranch date trees and tamarisks prosper, watered by the springs from Furnace Creek Wash.

In his *Illustrated Sketches of Death Valley*, John R. Spears tells of an almost fatal experience in the early eighties. Superintendent Perry, of the Pacific Coast Borax Company, and a companion started out one morning in a buggy to seek a better route for the borax wagons. The horse collapsed shortly, and died after they had worked over him for six or seven hours in the hot sun. Left afoot with only a canteen and half a pailful of water, the men waited until the sun had set and then in the slightly cooler air started up Wingate Wash. They hoped to reach a small wagon that stood in Wingate Pass, rest in its shade during the burning heat of the following day, and go on to Hidden Springs during the second night. On the way they agreed to take only tiny drinks, to make the water last, but one time when Perry was holding the canteen to his mouth he heard a rattlesnake whizz beside him and executed a rapid backward jump. The snake missed him, but Perry stumbled on some rocks and spilled almost all of the precious water. The two men reached the wagon in Wingate Pass just as the rising sun began to intensify in the heat. With the little water left in the canteen they moistened their tongues and throats at long intervals, trying to keep their throats from swelling shut and their tongues from swelling until they protruded beyond their lips. All day long the lay motionless in the small shaded rectangle beneath the wagon. All that endless day Perry, who came from Mississippi, saw the levee along the river and an old Negro selling watermelons; he could see himself 'tearing out the juicy red heart and putting it cool and dripping in my mouth.' Undoubtedly the arrival of a wagon late in the afternoon saved their lives, for by that time they were too weak to have gone on to Hidden Springs. It is said that Perry sat up till midnight, drinking water.

These two were fortunate—many others have been found dead in Death Valley. Not all of those who have died in the desert had exhausted their water supply, but more than one met death trying to dig for water with bare hands. The heat engendered in the body by the sun is like the fever created by infection, and is sometimes accompanied with delirium. A heart weakened by violent pumping of the blood to the surface of the body, and further exhausted by panic-stricken rushing about, suddenly stops. The summer traveler is advised to proceed cautiously. There is now no danger even during the hottest summer weather to motorists who stay on the main-traveled roads, which are regularly patrolled by park rangers. (See General Information.) [Ed. Note: Perhaps *little* danger is more accurate.]

Flora

Though in contrast with a verdant land Death Valley seems completely barren, it has a scattered vegetation of great variety. Saltgrass tinges the white lower levels, the covillea, or creosote bush, waves from the salt belt to the frost line; and mesquite thickets mark the Valley with green. There are many shrubs; several varieties of cactus; herbaceous plants with a brief blooming season; annuals which in a wet year tint the ground with delicate color; and, in the higher parts of the mountains, trees. In all, more than five hundred and sixty species of native plants have been found.

For life and growth, plants must take in a little more water than they evaporate. In the intense heat of Death Valley plants learn to meet

Pickleweed

this need in a number of ways. Their root systems are often extensive and intricate. Some of the cactuses spread their roots eighteen feet, only three inches below the surface, to absorb as much of the infrequent rains as possible, and mesquite has been known to send roots more than one hundred feet in search of water. Plant leaves are variously formed to retain moisture. Some are so minute as to be almost non-existent; others drop off with the coming of hot weather. The cactus leaves are thorns, the creosote bush leaves are covered with a varnish, and many other plants have dense growths of hairs.

Shrubs are widely spaced and, being completely exposed to the light, are round in form. A great many of them are whitish gray, with yellow flowers. The lovely desert holly grew much more profusely before many cars had left the Valley with entire plants crammed in between the fender and the hood. The Park Nursery is re-establishing this plant, but it may never again be plentiful on the gravel fans. In the spring its leaves grow thicker and are tinged with green, and its rudimentary flowers are yellowish-green. After the blooming season the leaves turn a beautiful silver gray; the seeds are faintly red. A shrub that rivals it in beauty is Death Valley sage, found in shaded canyons. It has slender, whitish intertwining stems, with delicate purplish blue flowers and tiny white powder-puff seedcases at the same time. The creosote bush, also called *covillea* in honor of Doctor Frederick Vernon Coville, member of the Death Valley Botanical Party of 1891 and author of a Death Valley Botany that is still standard, is one of the shrubs most frequently encountered, with slender, whiplike stems covered with brown bark, and bright green, shiny leaves that fall in the winter. In the spring it is covered with lightly poised yellow flowers, which are replaced by downy seedcases. In Daylight Pass the indigo bush blooms in the late spring; its deep blue, pea-shaped flowers, tiny dark green leaves, and almost white stems make it one of the most beautiful plants of the Valley. The odd paperbag bush scatters its swollen calyxes over the desert. A bright green bush with yellow flowers in spring is spruce bush, or desert fir, often found in canyons and washes. Cassia is a twiggy bush, covered solidly with yellow flowers in the spring. There are several varieties of encelia, often called brittlebush because of its brittle white stems; its daisy-shaped flowers are yellow. The desert, or Mormon, tea, a gray or pale green, jointed shrub with minute, scalelike leaves, has been used trustingly by both prospectors and Indians as a health drink.

Flowers in Death Valley, like desert blooms elsewhere, have a delicacy of form and purity of color that make hothouse blooms appear vulgarly lush. In a normally dry year, with an inch to an inch and a half of rain, the annuals are scarce and tiny, from two to six inches tall. But they mature and sow their seeds, and in a wet year, when from two to four inches of rain fall, they bloom in sheets, growing from eight to eighteen inches tall. There are nine varieties of pretty evening primroses. The golden evening primrose and the creamy, brown-eyed evening primroses are sweet-scented by day, but the silvery moon rose perfumes the air at night. Sand verbena is a sticky, trailing plant with clusters of small, fragrant, pinkish lavender flowers. The tiny desert gold poppy is a miniature edition of the California Poppy. A still smaller one, with petals sometimes only one-eighth of an inch long, is a delight to the finder. Curly-bloom, or desert heliotrope, grows blue, violet, purple, lavender, and white. Desert ghost is a tall white daisy, borne by gray stems that show faintly against the gravel, and the charming desert star is a low-growing white daisy. Whispering bells is a yellow flower that clings to the stem when dry and rustles in the wind.

Perennial herbaceous plants are widely scattered, Wetleaf has leaves that are always stickily damp to the touch. Honeysweet, a white, woolly bush with tiny yellow flowers, blooms in the autumn. Desert trumpet, sometimes called cigarette plant, has hollow stems that swell below the small flower; in winter these stems break at the top and curl back. The bear poppy has beautiful pure white flowers, one to three inches across. The Panamint daisy sends up its brilliant yellow flowers on stems three feet tall, the blossoms sometimes six inches across, and the tulip-shaped flowers of the desert mariposa (Sp.: *butterfly*) lily are orange-scarlet.

Mesquite and screw bean, the two trees found profusely in the Valley, have thorny branches and much-divided leaves; they grow in thickets wherever there is enough water. Cottonwoods and willows are found in near springs and in well-watered canyons. In Warm Spring

Bristlecone Pine, Telescope Peak

Canyon is a rankly growing group of fig trees, planted forty years ago; summer heat dries the fruits while they are still small, and they fall from the trees with the thud of pebbles. Piñons, or nut pines, providing food for the Indians, grow high on the Panamints, and the Grapevines. In the same regions are juniper, mountain mahogany, Rocky Mountain maple, and bristlecone and limber pine.

Cactuses are widely scattered on slopes above Death Valley and in the mountains. The *Opuntia echinocarpa* is a jointed gray variety. The *Echinocactus polycephalus* is a small barrel cactus, growing in clumps; in spring the upper thorns turn a vivid rose-red, and after the lovely flowers are gone the tops show seeds, encased in cotton, that are used for food by the Indians. The flat-jointed, spineless beaver-tail cactus is the *Opuntia basilaris*, which bears large magenta-pink flowers on the lobes. The calico cactus, *Echinocereus engelmanni*, has cylindrical stems and varicolored spines. There are seven other varieties, less often found.

Around the edges of the salt and alkali beds in the lowest levels of Death Valley are plants that cannot exist without this seasoning. Iodine bush, an odd, jointed plant, has the most appetite for this fare; then, in the order of lessening need, are the desert saltgrass, arrowweed, Cooper rush, and alkali sacaton, a coarse, nutritious grass. Bush seepweed and saltbush make up the outer ring, fading into the creosote-bush territory.

Fauna

Birds are the most noticeable form of animal life in Death Valley, and approximately one hundred and sixty varieties have been observed in the part below sea level. Many of the southern California birds have been seen here at one time or another, but the permanent residents are the most numerous and interesting. Ravens float and circle overhead and croak hoarsely; the road runner, crested, long-legged, and long-tailed, runs swiftly along the road or searches in the bushes for insects or lizards; the killdeer wades the pools of Badwater and Saratoga Springs in search of bugs and beetles; busy rock wrens are found from the low Valley floor to the tip of Telescope Peak; coveys of Gambel's quail scurry about the Furnace Creek Ranch, and mountain

Sparrow Hawk *Sharp-shinned Hawk*

Egret

quail and mourning doves live around the springs of the Panamints and the Funerals.

Besides these permanent residents, a great variety of bird life, similar to that of other mountainous regions of California, is seen in the wooded sections of the high Panamints. Ducks and geese come through the Valley every winter, and some settle at Saratoga Springs. Warblers, fly-catchers, sparrows, robins, and mockingbirds spend part of the winter here. In the spring, western meadow larks carol lustily. On warm nights motorists unacquainted with the 'poorwill are startled when what seems to be only a dusty rag on the road turns ruby eyes toward the car and surprisingly hurtles into the air.

Hundreds of species of insects live in the Death Valley area, supplying birds and lizards with food. Except for the inch-long horsefly (encountered only in hot weather), which draws blood when it bites, most of the insects are very unobtrusive. Butterflies, some of rare beauty, appear in the spring when the flowers bloom. In the evening bats circle and swoop about the electric lights, feeding luxuriously on flying insects; in the daytime they sleep in caves, or in abandoned mine tunnels.

But there are other inhabitants besides the insects and the birds.

A lacework trail cut by a tiny creature.

Tiny fat antelope ground squirrels, busy tails curved over their backs, race across roads and scutter from bush to bush. Small mice and kangaroo rats live in the sand dunes and mesquite thickets, where a lacework of trails radiates from the burrows, and the ground around is almost covered with discarded seedcases. Pack rats build untidy nests of sticks, to which they carry odds and ends picked up in strange places. They are honest traders, though, for they leave a pebble or a stick in exchange for the bit of bread, or any other small article, they take. Occasional desert coyotes and kit foxes roam the roads at night, and there are also wildcats, bobcats, badgers, and gophers.

A large herd of wild burros lives on the marsh near the Eagle Borax Works, and small bunches forage in the mountains or canyons. Many are descendants of animals that escaped from prospectors; sleek, alert, and happy, they are reverting in type to the ass introduced by the Spanish.

But the largest, most spectacular animal, though seldom seen, is the shy Nelson bighorn sheep, a variety of bighorn sheep inhabiting the great mountain range that runs through Canada, the United States, and Mexico. To the untutored eye he looks more like a goat than a sheep, for his hair is short and straight, dark brown on the back, shading to fawn on the under parts; and the eyes are golden. The most distinctive feature, the horns of the ram, curve in a graceful arc back toward the shoulder, then down and forward; the horns are about three feet long when fully developed. Ewes have short horns, only slightly curved. In bands the sheep roam the mountains, notably the northern Panamints, and come down into the canyons for water. They are extremely agile; when encountered in a canyon they pause for a brief look and then go up almost perpendicular slopes as effortlessly as flies walking up a wall.

All over the Valley floor, and up on the mountains in summer, are lizards of many species, sizes, and colors. The gridiron lizard darts about, his tail curled over his back; horned toads, when caught and scratched under the throat, stick out their chins and all but purr in enjoyment; the dull brown or olive chuckwalla, one of the largest lizards found in the United States, is ferocious in appearance but gentle in disposition.

Snakes are rarely seen. Down in the Valley is the sidewinder, twelve

Bighorn Sheep

to eighteen inches long, so called because it proceeds in a series of arcs instead of a simple wriggle. It lives in holes, hiding from summer heat and winter cold, but is sometimes met on the roads during warm nights. The Panamint rattler, a local variation, prefers higher elevation.

Even fish are found in Death Valley at Salt Creek and Saratoga Springs. They are tiny killifish, *Cyprinodon macularis*, not much more than an inch in length, survivors of the days when Death Valley held a lake.

History

Indians The Indians living in the Death Valley region when the white man came were of Shoshonean Comanche stock, dark and thickset, not very different from those living here today (1938). The early Indians told the white people that they were called Panamints; the range directly west of Death Valley was named for them. Today the Indians are usually called Shoshone.

It seems impossible that human beings could have found the means of supporting life in this barren area, but one or two hundred at a time did manage to do it. Their lives were conditioned by the search for food over much the same circuit year after year, following the lines of ripening vegetation. Grass seeds, piñon nuts, and mesquite beans were the chief foodstuffs, but no form of animal, or vegetable life was scorned. Some green-leaved plants were eaten, though repeated washings and boilings were required to remove their bitterness. Lobes of cactus were prepared by rolling them in the sand to remove their spines and then by boiling or drying. The Indians snared birds and rabbits, or shot them with arrows, and caught mice and lizards—chuckwallas were the prize catches. Even grasshoppers and grubs were eaten. Bighorn sheep were so much prized that the community united to build stone walls at strategic points to cut off escape; the animals were driven into these walled-off areas and slaughtered. It is reported that thirty sheep were taken in this way in 1891.

The winters were spent near springs. Though cave walls would have cut off the cold winds, the Indians chose to shiver through the cold months in crude brush shelters, because they believed that evil spirits had pre-empted the caves.

These Shoshone do not make pottery; shards of crude pots, probably obtained from other tribes, have been found at many of their old camps. The women still weave beautiful baskets from split shoots of willow and sumac, and decorate them with black from the horn-shaped pods of the unicorn plant. The red used in some of the coarser baskets comes from the roots of the Joshua tree, which grows south and west of Death Valley. In the past cooking baskets were lined with piñon pitch; red-hot rocks were thrown into water in them to make it boil. The arrowheads of these Indians were cleverly fashioned, usually

46

The art of basket making is handed down from one generation to another.

of obsidian—quail arrows about an inch long are delicate and beautiful; skinning knives were made of flint. Many broken and imperfect arrowheads are found in the dune of Mesquite Flat near the mouth of Cottonwood Canyon, where the Indians used to sit in the shade of the bushes while making them. Petroglyphs made by chipping the desert varnish from rocks, and drawings in red and black, are found in a number of canyons and caves. Some of the designs are undecipherable; a few represent men, deer, sheep, lizards, and turtles. The modern

Shoshone do not understand the pictures, nor do they know who made them.

Although other Indians have numerous superstitions, only a few have been discovered among these Shoshone. The Death Valley Indians believe that a house should be built to face the rising sun. They also believe that when one of them dies, his body must quickly be removed through a small opening made for the occasion—one that can be clapped shut before the spirit can rush back; otherwise the hut must be burned, which was probably a good sanitary practice in the days when the Indians lived in brush shelters. Today every adobe house in the Indian Village has a three-foot section of uncemented wall through which a body can be removed. [Ed. Note: This assertion cannot be verified today.] An old custom, possibly still in force, demanded that a medicine man who lost more than two patients should die. When the only son of Bill Shakespeare, a dignified old Shoshone who worked at Scotty's Castle, sickened, a medicine man was called in, but the boy died. In a great surge of grief and wrath, Shakespeare, who believed he was too old to have more children, took his shotgun and spent three weeks in the Grapevines, hunting the medicine man; he was unsuccessful, however, for the medicine man, well frightened, had moved to Arizona.

Early White Visitors White men long shunned this region; even the map made in 1847 and referred to during the treaty negotiations between the United States and Mexico in 1848 showed the Valley as part of the Great Basin.

In April of 1844 a party headed by John C. Frémont and guided by Kit Carson crossed from the San Joaquin Valley through Walker Pass in the southern Sierra Nevada during their search for a new route to Salt Lake City. They had swung southwest and found a river, which Frémont called Mohhahve for the local Indians. The party then picked up the old Spanish Trail, which they had been seeking, followed it to the Amargosa River, and pushed on to Hernandez Spring, known today as Resting Spring, a few miles east of Death Valley at the base of the Nopah Range. Frémont and his men thus skirted the southern end of Death Valley.

But the first whites to pass through Death Valley and to give it its

Early prospector

sinister name were a party of gold seekers and settlers who crossed it in '49. Their disastrous story was told by Lewis Manly, a survivor, in *Death Valley in '49*, a vivid description of wagon-train life and of suffering and death in a desolate land. [Ed. Note: Actually, William Lewis Manly.]

In September of 1849 a wagon train left Salt Lake City with Jefferson Hunt of the Mormon Battalion as its guide. Hunt said he would take the party over a new southern route that avoided the Salt Desert, where many travelers had come to disaster. There were in that train approximately 200 persons, 110 wagons, and 500 horses and oxen. Captain Hunt was to receive ten dollars a wagon for his services. The train rolled slowly south, ten miles a day. The immigrants had heard of a shorter way west and complained of the months this southern route would cost them, precious time lost from the gold fields. Some had read Frémont's book describing his trip from California to Salt Lake City; others had heard that Captain Joe Walker had guided a wagon train from Salt Lake City to a lake in Nevada (that later bore his name), then down Owens Valley and through the pass that Frémont had named for Walker. When another party caught up with the first and displayed a map that vaguely indicated Walker's route, the immigrants' wrath boiled over. Near Mountain Meadows in

Nevada, party after party broke off and swung to the west, the owners sure that they could find their way without a guide. Many returned to follow the tracks of the main party a few days later, when the country they had attempted to cross became impassable. Discussion of a shorter route, however, did not die. There were arguments and fights. Again the train swung west, leaving only seven wagons to follow Captain Hunt. When the westbound wagons were halted by a narrow canyon, feeling still ran high. Two men sawed in half the wagon they owned jointly, because neither hothead would give in to the other as to the route. The party divided once more; in the end the majority turned back to rejoin Hunt and the few that had gone on with him. They overtook Hunt and reached San Bernardino after an arduous trip.

Among those who had stubbornly continued west were three groups. The Jayhawkers, thirty young men from Illinois, found a route though the mountains for their twenty wagons. A man named Brier, with his wife and their three small boys, pulled out after them; the Jayhawkers resented this addition to their party but the Briers refused to leave them. The last group, the Bennett-Arcane party, was made up of two women, four children, and thirteen men—among them Manly. After some scouting about, the three parties turned in the same direction and traveled in loose contact, sometimes camping together. Lewis Manly, who later wrote the Death Valley saga, did not have a wagon to drive, but ranged ahead each day, hunting water to camp by and a route that the wagons could travel. It was not difficult to keep ahead of a train that could travel only ten miles a day at best.

The travelers slowly worked their way through the rough mountains, and then for weeks crawled across the upland deserts, a little cloud of dust in the vast expanse. Springs were few and the fall rains did not come as early as usual; cattle feed was scarce. The way grew rougher; each time a mountain was breasted another range was seen ahead.

One day Manly, disheartened, reported that an immense plain lay ahead with no signs of water; although a snowy mountain was in sight on its far side and he could see what looked like a pass, he did not believe they would be able to reach it. There was nothing, however, they could do but keep on; the way back was too long. The Jayhawkers

Death Valley

Early pioneers crossed Death Valley's unforgiving terrain.

decided on a final burst of speed to reach the pass, sure that the rich valleys of California must lie just beyond it. But the Bennetts and the Arcanes, hoping to find water along the way, decided to continue southward for a while.

For five days the Jayhawkers fought their way across the waterless plain. A fall of snow gave them respite and on the following day they reached the Amargosa River. Both stock and men drank the bitter water; the men did not know that the bitterness was caused by Epsom and Glauber's salts, though they were soon to learn it to their further distress. Weak and exhausted they reached what is now called Furnace Creek, where for the first time in many weeks they had more water than they could drink. Refreshed and strengthened, they urged their oxen down the wash, only to find—not the rich California lands they had hoped for, but the barren desolation of a narrow, salt-encrusted valley surrounded by towering ranges.

Moving more slowly than the Jayhawkers, the seven wagons of the Bennett-Arcane party went down a long, dry valley in Nevada, today named Emigrant Valley, between the Skull Mountains and the Spotted Range, and crossed the Amargosa Desert, where they picked up the Jayhawker trail not far from Furnace Creek Wash. Manly, moving

51

ahead down the wash, on Christmas Day found the Briers by the springs in Furnace Creek Wash. The children sat forlornly sucking bits of bacon rind, while their father, a clergyman, discoursed to them on the beauties of education. The Briers, traveling alone, had made a halt in Forty-Mile Canyon in Nevada, some twenty miles east of Beatty, had burned their broken wagons, and had loaded their possessions on their oxen. "It was a mistake," Mrs. Brier wrote later, "as we were about five hundred miles from Los Angeles and had only our feet to take us there."

From the Brier camp, Manly followed the trail of the Jayhawkers to their camp near Salt Creek. He found the formerly self-confident Jayhawkers badly frightened. They had decided to abandon their wagons and equipment and proceed on foot. The meat of their slaughtered oxen was drying over fires made from the wagons. (Bits of iron and burned wood were found here later.) Doty, their captain, told Manly that they intended to divide their food equally, and then it would have to be each man for himself. Young and strong, Manly was sure his best chance of surviving was to go with the Jayhawkers, but he also was sure that without his help the Bennetts and Arcanes would perish; and so he went back to them. On the way he met two of the men from his party who had decided to join the Jayhawkers. One of these Manly was to see again—dead in the Slate Range.

The Jayhawkers started up Emigrant Wash and crossed the Panamints, planning to go west and then south; the Briers trailed after them. Moving in small parties over the rugged mountains west of Death Valley, they had almost incredible meetings with one another. Some of the older men, unable to endure the exhaustion of hunger and thirst, died on the way, but the others, without guide or trail, stumped doggedly on till they reached Los Angeles.

After Manly had rejoined them, the wagons of the Bennett-Arcane party rolled slowly down Furnace Creek Wash, the oxen so feeble they could hardly pull the wagons down the rough grade. Ahead was the snowy mountain Manly had seen, but the immigrants could not see any pass. They tried to go south around the tall, steep mountains, but the oxen could not drag the wagons over the rough salt. So the party crossed to the west side of the Valley and forced the wagons up a long wash into a canyon of the Panamints in the hope that they could surmount them there. A cliff ended that attempt. They toiled back down to the floor of the Valley. An ox died on the way. Four men deserted to follow the Jayhawkers on foot. The pitiable little group camped in exhaustion and despair; their food was almost gone, the scanty water was bitter, and the Valley was hemmed in by steep mountain barriers. It was finally decided that Manly and John Rogers should go ahead alone to find a way out and bring back food. Bennett believed that at the longest they would be back in fifteen days. An ox was killed, so poor and thin that it took seven-eighths of its dried flesh to fill the two knapsacks. The two men started in the early morning, and those left behind waved hats and bonnets to them as they diappeared from sight.

For a few days the party rested in the Valley. Then the single men, both those restless with their own wagons and the drivers of the Arcane wagons, became restless. They doubted that Manly and Rogers would be so foolish as to return; they said that when the oxen were gone they would all die. Before long they too left to follow the Jayhawkers. Only two families with four little children remained here. Captain Culverwell, one of the men who left, changed his mind somewhere on the trail and started back to the Bennett camp; he was later found dead, on his back with outstretched arms, not far from the camp of those he had deserted. Not a morsel of the food he had carried was left, and the two little powder cans he had taken to hold water were dry.

The Bennetts and Arcanes, anxiously awaiting deliverance, had only a little rice and tea left with which to vary the meals of stringy ox meat. At night they dreamed of crusty loaves of fresh bread, and woke to hear their children crying in hunger. The two-year-olds, Charlie Arcane and Martha Bennett, suffered most from the restricted diet; little Martha, who had been able to climb in and out of the wagons so spryly that she reminded Manly of a quail, became sick. Lacking medicine and medical aid, her parents had no hope that she would live. But her fever finally waned, and, though pitifully thin, she did recover.

The allotted fifteen days passed after the departure of Manly and Rogers, but neither returned; though the others had little hope, Bennett firmly believed that Manly would come back if he were alive.

Days dragged on. Determined to make a last attempt before they died, the members of the party prepared to leave. The wagons, they decided, must be left; the remaining oxen should be used to carry the women and children. The men tore the canvas tops from the wagons to make pack harnesses and the women sewed two hickory shirts together to form saddle-bags that would hold the two small children.

They worked slowly, with little hope, sitting in the shade of the wagons. Charlie and Martha fretted, and Melissa and George played listlessly with their few toys and with Cuff, the dog. Manly and Rogers had been gone twenty-five days when the desert stillness was broken by a crash. In the silence that closed in again after the shot, the travelers scrambled from beneath the wagons. Not far away was Manly holding a smoking gun, and Rogers leading a little black mule with a pack on its back. Bennett, Arcane, and Mrs. Bennett rushed towards the scouts to embrace them hysterically. As they walked back to the wagons, Manly said, "they stopped two or three times, and turned as if to speak, but there was too much feeling for words; convulsive weeping would choke the voice."

As Manly unpacked flour and beans from the mule he told them that he and Rogers had crossed more than two hundred miles of desert mountains and found a "native Californian" ranch, thirty miles from Los Angeles. The people there had fed them and sold them some food and two horses for thirty dollars; they had bought the mule and another horse from a freight train. But the horses had not been able to endure the rough, waterless going on the way back to Death Valley; one had died, and the other two had become so weak the men had had to leave them in a canyon. The little mule, on the contrary, had trudged on, nosing out water, snatching at every bit of green.

Among other things Manly took four yellow balls from a sack and handed one to each child; these, the first oranges the children had seen, had been sent to them by the Mexican woman at the ranch.

After a few delicious meals of bread and beans, the little train started out of the Valley with Rogers leading the mule, and the oxen following; Charlie and Martha stood in the hickory shirt pockets hung across the back of Old Crump, and George and Melissa sat on his back. Each woman rode an ox. Mrs. Arcane, wearing her best dress and beribboned hat, made a brave appearance until a strap on the ox slipped and he began bucking and bawling. The other animals caught the excitement and bounced about, shaking off their packs. Someone snatched the children to safety, but Mrs. Arcane, with ribbons and skirts flying, clung desperately to her seat until the ox bucked her to the ground. When the men found that she was not hurt, they rolled on the ground, holding their sides and whooping hysterically. It had been long since any of them had laughed.

The travelers camped for the night and the next morning reloaded with care. When the party reached the top of the Panamints on the second day, it halted and the men climbed a peak to look back at the brilliantly colored mountains and shimmering valley floor where they had spent a bitter month. Someone said, "Good-bye, Death Valley." It has borne the name ever since.

The travelers struggled down the Panamints, up over the Slate Range, each night dropping asleep in exhaustion. The rough, steep course seemed endless, but they now saw that their plight was not hopeless. On the ninth day Manly announced, "Half-way." One day they made only a few miles—a snowstorm on the Mojave chilled their thin blood, mud sucked at their feet. Finally only one range lay between them and a stream Manly and Rogers had found; but it was covered with soft snow so that the weak oxen could not struggle through. That night the party camped with a feeling of despair, but the snow hardened in the night, and on the following morning they were able to descend into California. The dreadful journey was nearly over.

The roads these foolhardy people took cannot be definitely determined. Few traces of their passage through the desert have been found, and members of the party who went back in later years could not agree on the way they had come, because the tumbled desert mountains look much alike.

To the coast with the Death Valley sojourners came not only a tale of the dreadful barren wastes, but also a story of a glittering piece of rock, picked up near Death Valley; it was widely told that a gunsmith, to whom the rock had been taken for use as a front sight of a gun, had declared that the ore was solidly veined with silver. The finder then "remembered" that he had seen a whole hill of this rock, but though he made several trips to Death Valley, he never found what became known as Gunsight Mine, a lodestar of propectors for many years.

The first party to search for the Gunsight was that of Dr. Darwin French, who left Oroville with about a dozen companions in the spring of 1860. They rode down the San Joaquin Valley, through Walker Pass, and found some mines at Coso, forty-five miles west of Death Valley. From there French's party went on, discovering and naming Darwin Falls, Panamint Valley, and the Panamint Range. From Panamint Valley they climbed a canyon to what they called Towne's Pass, for a member of the 1849 immigrant party. The men then descended into Death Valley, where they saw the creek and wash which they named Furnace—it was then the hot season. They went as far south as Bennett's Well, which they named for Asa Bennett of the 1849 party. Though French and his companions saw a great deal of the Death Valley country and christened many spots, they did not find the legendary mine.

In the fall of 1860 Dr. S. A. George and Dr. Lilley, members of French's party, and four other men started from Visalia, bound for Death Valley and the Gunsight. Their experiences paralleled those of the French expedition. They named Rose Spring, today called Wildrose Spring, and Telescope Peak, and found a few small mineral deposits, but did not find the Gunsight Mine. In 1861 George returned, ran a tunnel on his claim in Wildrose Canyon, and left four men to work it; but they were killed by Indians and no further operations were attempted.

Jacob Breyfogle, a blacksmith of Austin, Nevada, made a prospecting trip into the Death Valley region in 1864. He returned in poor mental condition, with a tale for having been mistreated by the Indians and with several pieces of rock, rich in free gold. He could never again find the place where he had been, though he tried several times, as did others. So, to the lost Gunsight Mine was added the lost Breyfogle Mine; no trace of either has ever been found. The rich ore exhibited by those who reported the finds may have been float (ore washed down from a vein at a higher elevation) or it may have come from a pocket (an isolated deposit, usually small).

In the following years, when any area might yield a strike, men filtered into the region from the west and north, and from Nevada. There were other visitors, too; the near-by country provided an excellent hideout for men too rough and too tough even for the

A misspelled trace of the lost Breyfogle Mine.

roistering frontier camps. Many moved into the high Panamints, which have game, water, and firewood. The first official inhabitant of Death Valley itself was Bellerin Tex Bennett, who settled at a pleasant sport irrigated by water from Furnace Creek and raised alfalfa, barley and quail.

In 1870 an official expedition of approximately sixty men was sent here under the command of Lieutenants Wheeler and Lyle, to report on the country. They made two trips, one through Saline Valley to the northern end of Death Valley, and the other through Darwin Wash and Wildrose Canyon, to cross Death Valley and continue east to Ash Meadows. These trips were made during the hottest part of the year. Two guides from Independence disappeared and were not heard of again, though they knew the country well.

A more successful Government expedition was that led by Lieutenant Rogers Birnie, Jr., in 1875. The party climbed over the Panamints, camped at Bennett's Well, and crossed the salt beds over what Birnie referred to as "the old emigrant road to Furnace Creek"—the trail that Manly and Bennett had made sixteen years before.

The most picturesque period in Death Valley was the mining days. There were a number of discoveries, from Panamint in 1874 to

Early survey party, July 1939

Rhyolite in 1906, with towns springing up by them, living briefly, then dying. Between 1906 and 1920 hardly anyone thought of Death Valley without also thinking of one man—Death Valley Scotty (born Walter Scott). Heat and distances had no terrors for him. He and his mule wandered and explored, and he was very mysterious about his mines.

By 1918 automobiles were appearing fairly frequently in Death Valley, bouncing over rocks that ripped tires and tore off oil pans and differentials and traveling only about fifteen miles an hour, but traveling none the less. At that the visitors had less trouble than an adventurous party from Tonopah that in 1906 visited the Valley in a Pope-Toledo and mired it in the soggy marsh near Salt Creek; the passengers finally had to run along beside the car, throwing caps and coats under the churning wheels, in order to free it and keep it moving. As a final desperate measure they threw lumps of salt at the hesitant chauffeur, yelling wildly that he must not stop and must keep the throttle pulled far down until the car could reach firm ground and safety. Those who like a dash of adventure and want solitude can still find roads in Death Valley where the going is somewhat rough; but unless such romanticists are as imprudent as the first white visitors to the region, they run no risks of danger or prolonged discomfort. Prior to the creation of the Death Valley National Monument in 1933, the Pacific Coast Borax Company, operating the hotels, camps, service stations, at Death Valley Junction and Furnace Creek, performed most of the functions now exercised by the National Park Service. This company has contributed largely to the development of the region. Many of the place names, such as Zabriskie Point, perpetuate the memory of the company's pioneer employees.

Borax

In the seventies, when borax was used only as a drug, producers got fifty cents a pound for it. The principal sources in this country were the white borax marshes of California and Nevada, where it was cooked and crystallized into a pure product.

Aaron and Rosie Winters lived in a little stone dugout at Ash Meadows, near Las Vegas, Nevada. Winters was in his sixties and his wife was frail; all they had gained from his years of prospecting were this one-room dugout, a few chickens, and a pig. One night a prospector stopped for the night with them and, in the course of talk on prospects, told them of borax and its value, describing the marshes where it was found, and explained a simple test producing a green flame and identifying borax.

The next day, after the visitor had left, Winter, who had been in Death Valley and remembered that its marshes were like those the prospector had described, threw a pack on a burro and started off with his wife. Spurred by dreams of wealth they punched the burro from Ash Meadows to Death Valley, through Furnace Creek Wash, and to a spot several miles beyond. There they gathered "cotton balls" from the marsh, crushed the fibrous, woolly stuff, and impatiently waited for dark. When night wrapped the Valley, Winters poured chemicals over the crushed material, and shaking with excitement, held a match to the mixture. As a flame trembled over the saucer, he shouted, "She burns green, Rosie! We're rich, by God!"

In 1881 Winters sold his borax-marsh claims to W.T. Coleman for $20,000, most of which went into a big ranch at Pahrump, Nevada; Rosie died there a few years later.

In 1880, when Isidore Daunet heard that Winters had found borax in Death Valley, he recalled his trip there in the summer of '75 and organized the Eagle Borax Works. This company crystallized some borax, but the low-grade product sold for so little that the enterprise was abandoned.

In 1881 the Harmony Borax Works were built about five miles north of Furnace Creek, where Winters had found borax. For a year the product was freighted out by Charles Bennett of Pahrump Valley, but the company decided that it would be more economical to do its own freighting. Superintendent Perry, after studying wagons that hauled freight over the mountains and deserts of the West, designed a wagon with a capacity of ten tons. Ten were built—so stoutly constructed that they remained in service for five years without a breakdown. Two wagons, linked together as a lead and a trailer, were drawn by teams of twelve to twenty mules; the "wheeler" pair was usually horses. The lead pair of one of these jingling strings of twenty mules was harnessed one hundred feet in front of the lead wagon; the animals were controlled by profanity and a cotton jerk line, half an inch thick, that ran through a ring on one mule in each pair. If the driver wished the leaders to go to the right, he gave a steady pull; when he wished the team to go to the left, he jerked the line—hence the name. Two men, a driver and a swamper, handled each outfit; the

Early Death Valley Railroad car

F.M. "Borax" Smith

driver managed the animals, and the swamper did everything else, from cooking and washing up to putting on the brakes on the down grades and heaving rocks at the mules to encourage them on the up stretches. Because of the heat or the isolation, swampers and drivers frequently became irritated with each other. Although the company tried to change crews often enough to keep personnel intact, several men had their heads broken by shovels or by wagon spokes.

Water, naturally, was scarce on the long haul to Mojave. There were only three wells on the route in Death Valley itself; the first was at Eagle Borax Works, thirteen miles from the Harmony Station; the second, Bennett's Well, four miles beyond; and Mesquite Well, thirty-three miles away. Thirty-five miles farther came Windy Gap (now Wingate Pass); water for this station came from Hidden Spring, eight miles away in the Quail Mountains. The next water was at Lone Willow Spring, twenty-seven miles from Granite Wells. The longest waterless gap was the fifty miles between Granite Wells and Mojave. Stations were built about every sixteen miles, so that there would be camping places between the water stations at the points to which the teams could haul the heavily loaded wagons in one day. Each dry camp had a five-hundred-gallon-tank wagon of water for the thirsty men and animals, and two to four feed boxes, each holding four bales of hay and six sacks of barley, and refilled by returning crews in the borax wagons; these crews also replenished the tank wagons, pulling them to the nearest spring and back. Coming back from Mojave without a load of borax, the teams could travel more than sixteen miles a day, so there were additional stations for them. A round trip usuallly took thirty days. All hauling stopped, however, during the really hot weather between June 15 and September 15.

In 1887 such quantities of borax came in from Italy and the price dropped so low that the Death Valley works were closed. The twenty-mule team, however, had become identified with the product. Coleman's company was sold in 1889 to the Pacific Coast Borax Company, headed by F.M. (Borax) Smith. This company reopened operations in Death Valley in 1890, when a solid form of borax, named colemanite, was discovered along the north end of the Black Mountains. The Lila C. was the first mine worked; the settlement by it was called Ryan. Later Ryan was moved to its present position in the Black Mountains. Discovery of another type of borax on the Mojave Desert once again made the cost of production in Death Valley too high, and the mines at Ryan were closed in 1927.

Highway Tours

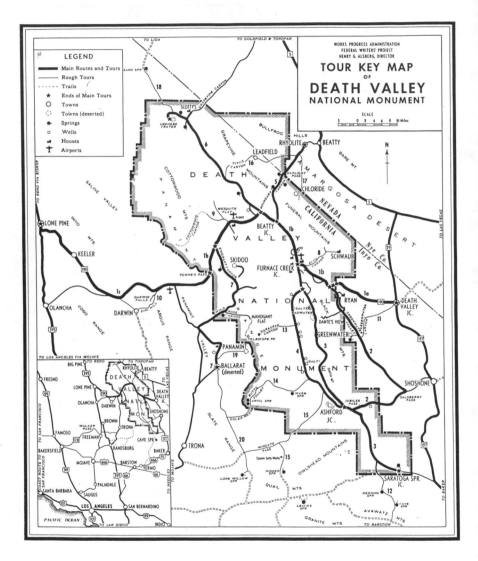

Tour 1:

Death Valley Junction, Calif.—Furnace Creek
Junction—Beatty Junction—Stove Pipe Wells—
Lone Pine, Calif.

139 m., Calif. 190

Update:

❖ "Oiled roadbed" is paved.

❖ Death Valley Junction (pop. 10) is owned by Marta Becket,
who also owns and operates the Amargosa Opera House
from October through May. The dancer-entrepeneur has
been profiled in many publications, including *National Geo-
graphic* and *People,* for her performances and Opera House,
which is complete with its own audience-murals. See Appendix for specific information.

❖ The red house in Twenty-Mule Team Canyon is now gone.

❖ Park at the Zabriskie Point parking area, and walk the .3 mile
up to the viewpoint.

❖ The old public garage located at the Furnace Creek Inn is no
longer open; there is a service station located near the Furnace Creek Ranch, along with store and restaurants.

❖ The elevation of Telescope Peak is 11,049 feet.

❖ Sunset and Texas Springs campgrounds are closed during the
summer months.

❖ Although some Tumbisha Shoshone still live in Death Valley,
they no longer maintain a trading post.

❖ Death Valley Airport has landing lights, but no hangars are
available today.

❖ The fish at Salt Creek are called pupfish; their Latin name is *Cyprinodon salinus.*

❖ Gnomes' Workshop was washed out in a flood many years ago, but is restoring itself today. (The name is said to have come from the distinctive "tink-tink" sound of the salt crystals drying in the sun, or from the gnomelike shapes of the alkaline formations.)

❖ The park nursery is now gone.

❖ CalTrans Maintenace facilities are located at Cow Creek.

❖ The Death Valley Visitor Center and Death Valley Museum are located just north of Furnace Creek. This extensive facility is the hub of activity in Death Valley, the National Park Service Headquarters and the major information outpost.

❖ There is a Ranger Station at Stovepipe Wells; there is no longer one at Emigrant Canyon Road. There is no fuel available at the gravel landing field. The campground at Stovepipe Wells is closed during the summer, but the Emigrant Campground is open.

❖ The road to Mosaic Canyon is recommended for 4WD only.

Oiled roadbed.

Sec. a   Death Valley Junction to Eastern Boundary of Monument, 17m.

The desert town of Death Valley Junction, Calif., is 96 miles north of Crucero, Calif., by the Tonopah and Tidewater R.R. and 80 miles north of Baker by Calif. 127. West of this little town, Calif. 190 climbs a long easy grade to a pass between two mountain ranges, and then descends to the eastern entrance of the Monument, following the natural path taken by the unfortunate immigrants in '49.

Death Valley Junction (alt. 2000; pop. 200); 0 m., at the junction of Calif. 127 and 190, was a bustling town when borax was being shipped from Ryan; today its inhabitants are chiefly employed in a large plant refining filter clay. A long, U-shaped building in the center of the town holds the post office, the store, the restaurant, and the Amargosa Hotel (rates, $2.50 up, European plan,). Two old Borax Wagons stand in the small plaza between the wings of the building; in the '80s, drawn by

66

The famed Amargosa Opera House

20-mule teams and laden with borax, they rolled between Death Valley and Mojave in clouds of dust.

West of Death Valley Junction the straight line of the highway ascends a slope toward the Black Mountains (L) whose creamy clay is thinly covered with dark brown rocks. The Funeral Mountains (R), gnarled and rough, rise abruptly from the slope; Pyramid Peak (alt. 6725) raises its blunt, angular tip from the southern end of the range, with zebra-like bandings that are an excellent example of the varicolored Paleozoic formations.

❖ The low pass to Death Valley, visible at 4.6 m., lies between the jagged, distorted siennas and umbers of the Funeral Mountains and the dark masses of the Black Mountains.

❖ West of the summit (alt 3042), 10 m., the highway crosses rolling upland country covered with desert brush, principally sage and creosote. The dark rocks of the Black Mountains (L) are coated with shiny dark brown "desert varnish," the result of the sun's long-continued action on their manganese content. It is this same action that, in this region, gives shades of purple to white glass. (Jam jars and bottles found in the wash below the Keane Wonder Mine had turned to a purple that was almost black.) The trestles (L) are remains of the abandoned railroad that carried borax from Ryan to the Junction.

❖ Descending through low mud cliffs, the highway reaches the boundary (alt. 2000), 17 m., of Death Valley National Monument.

Sec. b. Eastern Boundary Furnace Creek Wash—Beatty Junction—Western Boundary; 56 m., Calif. 190.

West of the Monument entrance, Calif. 190 descends the broad Furnace Creek Wash into the magnificence of central Death Valley. Turning north the road passes the oasis of Furnace Creek Ranch and runs into the low range of hills that bisects the Valley. North of these hills is the grandeur of the wide northern section of the Valley. The route crosses the salt marsh, curves around the Sand Dunes, and climbs the long grade up Emigrant Wash to Towne's Pass and the western entrance of Death Valley.

❖ West of the boundary (alt. 2000), 0 m., Calif. 190 descends Furnace Creek Wash. The Black Mountains (L) here have brilliant streaks of rose, green, and tan, below a lava-capped crest; delicately colored green and beige hills stand out against the gravel slopes below the mountains.

❖ A Ranger Checking Section (See General Information) is at 1 m.

❖ At 1.5 m. is a junction with the Dante's View-Greenwater Valley Road (See Tour 2).

As the road proceeds west, the blunt end of the Funeral Mountains is right, with hot tans and rosy browns, banded with somber gray. The angle of the strata in the Black Mountains (L) is noticeable, sloping gently up from the Amargosa Desert to present a blunt face to Death Valley.

❖ At 5.4 m. is the junction with a one-way road that loops back to Calif. 190.

> Left on this road through Twenty-Mule-Team Canyon, 0.2 m. The road winds and dips between low yellow clay hills, with Death Valley visible now and then. At 2.4 m. the low hills, resembling a herd of elephants, can be seen rolling away to the brilliant walls of the Black Mountains, whose tilted layers of rose, fawn, green, and tan are topped with a black lava cap. The red house at 2.5 m. was formerly a boarding house for teamsters and miners of the borax company. The hills are scarred with tunnels of old workings. The road rejoins Calif. 190 at 4.4 m.

❖ At 8.2 m. on Calif. 190 is the exit of the looping road (see above). Westward is an impressive view of Death Valley. Mountains, rugged and distorted, gouged by canyons from summit to base, rise above a smooth slope of detrital waste. Great spurs of the bordering ranges run down to the narrow white Valley floor. The western range is the Panamint, tan and dun with rose and purple overtones. North, beyond the low brown and yellow foothills of the Funeral Mountains, the concave arc of the range follows the curve of the Valley to the serrated profile of the blue Grapevine Mountains, 28 miles away. The dominating bulk of Tin Mountain (alt. 8900) is far up Death Valley; beyond a cream and chocolate butte at the end of the wash is Tucki (Ind.: *sheep*) Mountain (alt. 6705), smoothly outlined.

Cleanly sculptured hills lie on both sides of the highway, golden yellow (L) and brown (R).

❖ At 9.5 m. is a junction with an oiled road.

Left on this road, which terraces a small hill, to Zabriskie Point, 0.3 m. Rows of deeply folded yellow hills spread toward the nearby brilliant Black Mountains and fall away toward Death Valley. In Tertiary times the land forming these hills was a lake bed; it was long ago lifted and folded into the present form by violent earth movements. The sharp, golden peak (R) is Manly Beacon.

❖ At 10.7 m., on Calif. 190, is a junction with the Echo Canyon Road (see Tour 8).

The wash is dotted with sparse desert shrubs: the graceful creosote bush, with yellow flowers in spring; rounded bushes of gray desert holly; and bright green clumps of desert fir. In spring there are many bright flowers.

❖ Furnace Creek Springs (R), 11.4 m., are in a fresh green thicket. It was with this sweet water that the first unwilling visitors slaked their dusty throats in 1849, after an almost waterless five-day journey across the Amargosa Desert. The springs have a temperature of 70°; the water is carried by pipe line to the swimming pool at Furnace Creek Inn and to Furnace Creek Ranch.

❖ Furnace Creek Inn (at sea level), 12.6 m., is a large resort (rates from $7.75 up, American plan; outdoor swimming pool, fed by warm springs, tennis courts). Across the road from the inn is a garage, a service station and a store that sells soda, cigarettes, and the like.

❖ At 12.7 m. is a junction with oiled East Highway (see Tour 3).

West of the junction, Calif. 190 dips below sea level. The Valley here is broad, covered with sand and gravel, occasional bushes, and thickets of mesquite.

Telescope Peak (alt. 11,045) in the Panamints is southwest; throughout the winter it is covered with snow, and wears a small white cap late into May. The mountains are barbaric in color and their structure is distorted; but they have repose and serenity: in the early evening, their flamboyant coloring dies and they become a soft, transparent blue, but stand out sharply against the lighter blue of the sky.

❖ At 13.5 m. is a junction with a road.

> Right on this road 0.5 m. to the large Texas Springs Public Campground (water and sanitary facilities; stay limit 30 days), on a little bench overlooking the Valley. Parking sites are neatly marked off with rocks. The Park Service is planting native shrubs around the grounds to augment the mesquite that already grows here.

❖ Furnace Creek Camp (L), 13.8 m., is a moderately priced resort in the southeastern corner of Furnace Creek Ranch. (Rates from $1.50 up; sleeping and housekeeping cabins, store, restaurant, service station, Nov. 1-May 1; emergency accommodations in summer). Beside the road are a borax wagon, trailer, and a steam tractor used in the '80s. Borax Smith designed this iron tractor to supplant the 20-mule teams. He had a road surveyed to the line of the Union Pacific R.R. in Nevada, and intended to have the tractor haul the borax, but this project proved impracticable. The tractor was later sold to the Keane Wonder Mine for the hauling of ore, but it stuck on its first trip up Daylight Pass and stayed there for nearly 30 years before it was brought here. Burdick's *The Mystic Mid-Region*, which contains some fantastic misinformation about Death Valley, has a photograph of the tractor rolling down a road, with charming young ladies perched on it, dressed in the voluminous tailored skirts and dashing sailor hats of the gay '90s.

> Left from Furnace Creek Camp on a dirt road to a Ranger Station, 0.1 m.

The Indian Village, 0.7 m., is the home of 30 or so Indians. Squat adobes have been built for them by the Park Service, and a Trading Post at which baskets, jewelry, and other handicraft products are sold. These Shoshone wear modern garb, and a few own small cars. They are citizens, not wards of the Government, and earn their own living. Most of the men worked on Scotty's Castle; some are employed at Furnace Creek Ranch and by the Park Service.

❖ Furnace Creek Ranch (L) (alt. -178) 13.8 m., is irrigated by water piped from Furnace Creek. Bellerin V. Tex Bennett, the first man to live here, and probably the first white man to live in Death Valley, came here in 1870 with a few pairs of quail and the intention of growing alfalfa and barley. He left after a few years, when the Harmony Borax Works took over the "ranch." They grew acres of alfalfa to feed the mules, had a half-acre pond and a small orchard, and called the place Greenland. Its present name was given by the Pacific Coast Borax Company. Long rows of tamarisk were planted to break the hot

Harvesting dates

desert winds, and Washingtonia palms, whose bunchy tops can today be seen for miles, were set out. Today (1938) there is a flourishing plantation of date palms, whose crop is boxed for sale (50¢ a pound); a grassy golf course (see General Information) occupies the former alfalfa field; and descendants of Bellerin Tex's quail call to one another in the brush.

❖ Death Valley Airport (R), 14 m., is maintained by the Park Service (Private hangar for rent, gas and service at Furnace Creek Camp; see above.)

❖ The Ruins of the Harmony Borax Works, on a low bluff at 15.5 m., are visible (L). Adobe walls and rusty boilers and tanks are all that is left of the first borax works in Death Valley, established in the '80s. Water was piped from Furnace Creek, and adobe houses were built for the 40 men who worked here. Chinese gathered the "cotton balls" of borax from the marsh, and white men almost denuded the area of mesquite and creosote for fuel to heat the boiling pans. Workers seldom stayed here more than three months. One said, "Paiute ladies were the only women to visit us!" The works were operated for 5 years, and during this time borax was hauled out in huge wagons by the famous 20-mule teams. (See Borax.)

Waterfalls, Gnomes' Workshop

Gnomes' Workshop

❖ At 16.2 m. is a junction with a one-way dirt road looping back to the main route.

Left on this road, through Mustard Canyon, 0.7 m., to pass between the low mud hills of dull yellow that give the canyon its name. The salt crusted over the yellow surface looks like a sprinkling of snow.

❖ At 16.4 m. on the main highway is a junction with a dirt road.

Right on this road to a parking station, 0.2 m., left from the parking station on a short trail that leads down to the Gnomes' Workshop, where a tiny stream of bitter tasting water flows through acres of odd alkaline formations and tumbles over salt crystals in miniature waterfalls.

❖ At 17.3 m. on the main highway is a junction with an oiled road.

Right on this road to a junction with an oiled road, 0.2 m., left here 1.5 m. to the Park Nursery on Cow Creek. Many plants, particularly desert holly and mesquite, are cultivated here for use in a restoration of the native vegetation of the Valley. A large lath shelter protects other plants from the sun.

At Park Village, 1.6 m., the National Park Service personnel has its winter quarters.

On the main side road at 0.6 m. are the Headquarters of Death Valley National Monument. The area is administered under supervision from this office. Roads and trails are built and wells and springs are inspected and improved to provide a safe water supply. Much of the development work has been done by the Civilian Conservation Corps.

❖ At 25 m. on the main highway is a junction with the Daylight Pass Road (see Tour 5).

In the Salt Flats below the road, Salt Creek winds sluggishly, vivid blue in the sun. The inch-long Death Valley fish live here; prospectors amuse themselves by holding a pan full of crumbs just below the surface and watching the greedy fish crowd in to eat. They come so rapidly and in such numbers that they sometimes make small waves.

❖ At about 25 m. the route crosses a range of low hills into the northern part of the strange, barren valley. Directly north is the huge gravel fan from Boundary Canyon, with the Death Valley Buttes, triangular and dark, thrusting up from its surface.

❖ At 31 m. is a junction (R) with the road to Ubehebe Crater and to Scotty's Castle (see Tour 6).

The road curves sharply west (L) here across the Salt Marshes and

Devil's Cornfield

toward the Panamints. The roadbed is unusually bumpy, for water rising from below by capillary action keeps the salty earth moist and rough. Around the marsh is the Devil's Cornfield, where the arrow-weed resembles shocks of corn tied about the middle. The Jayhawkers camped near here in '49 before starting their final trek over the mountains. Bits of wood and old iron were found on the spot, where they burned their wagon in order to dry ox flesh to sustain them on the journey. This was about all they had to eat until they reached settled country.

West of the Salt Marshes the road runs below the wrinkled rose and umber sides of Tucki Mountain. The yellow Sand Dunes (R), rising in sharply sculptured lines, cover some 25 square miles. When the hot summer winds blow, the sand rises in a great swirling mass of yellow to fill the trough of Death Valley with a gritty fog that obscures sun and mountains. Around the edges of the dunes are mesquite, creosote, four-winged saltbush, and other desert shrubs; small rodents live here, marking the smooth dunes with a lacework of trails.

❖ Stove Pipe Wells Hotel (at sea level), 39 m., is a resort (rates from $2 up, European plan, hotel sleeping cabins, coffee shop, restaurant, gas station, emergency accommodations in summer); there is an Emergency Airport (fuel service only) a few hundred feet (R) from the highway. The old wagon by the gas station is the one responsible for the name Lost Wagons, 25 miles north on the Government topographical maps. The wagon, abandoned in the summer of 1889 when the horses could not pull it through the sand in the heat, was brought here in 1926, a reminder of the days when travel through Death Valley was difficult and perilous.

By the hotel is the junction (R) with a sandy road leading to Mesquite Flat and part way up to Cottonwood Canyon (see Tour 9).

❖ At 39.2 m. is a junction with a dirt road.

> Right on this road to Mosaic Canyon, 3 m. The bed of the canyon has been cut through conglomerate—small rocks and sand particles that were cemented together ages ago—by the gravel and sand tumbled out though thousands of years of flood water. The varicolored pebbles of the conglomerate have been worn to a smooth, mosaic-like surface that gives the canyon its name. The floor and walls a little farther on are masses of

Johnny Shoshone

polished buff marble. The upper part of the canyon has been made accessible to hikers by two ladders crossing dry waterfalls.

Between the bossy masses of Tucki and the tumbled slopes of the northern Panamints, the main highway climbs Emigrant Wash, named in memory of the people who panted up its slope in '49, fleeing from death. The tumbled strata of the Panamints (R) are evidence of the violent distortions this region has undergone.

The old Lemoigne Mine is beyond a ridge (R). Jean Lemoigne, a black-bearded Frenchman, had left his ship in the late 1870s, bound for the booming mining camp of Darwin, where he hoped to make a fortune with which he could retire and live pleasantly in Paris. In 1882 he filed a claim here on a piece of ground where the Indians scratched for lead, and where he found silver as well. He worked the claim, but made no large amount of money. During the mining boom in Rhyolite in 1906, he was offered $80,000 for his property, but the sum was in the form of a draft and he believed only in hard money. He refused the slip of paper, although the engineers offered to take him to Lone

Pine to cash it. For 11 years more he lived on at his mine with his burros and the Indians, still hoping for fortune. In June 1918, Scotty and Shoshone Johnny, an Indian, found his body lying under a mesquite tree on the old road near Salt Creek. Jean had tied his burros to a bush and they too were dead. Scotty and Shoshone Johnny buried him on the spot and put up a penciled board to mark the grave. Several years later when Edna Brush Perkins, author of *White Heart of Mojave* walked through Death Valley, Jean's coffeepot still stood beside his fireplace and the skeletons of the little burros were still tied to the mesquite.

❖ A Ranger Station (alt. 1542) (see General Information) is at 48.3 m. Here (L) is the junction with Emigrant Canyon Road (see Tour 7).

Southwest of the ranger station the road continues to climb the long alluvial fan of Emigrant Wash. Creosote bushes are large here and bloom earlier than those in the Valley. The flowers look like flocks of tiny yellow butterflies poised among the glittering leaves. The cactus here blooms in May, with flowers in rich tones of reds and purplish pinks. The higher levels of the Panamints are more gentle in aspect than the lower, and their tawny rock slopes are closely speckled with desert shrubs.

Among the tumbled peaks (L) is Jayhawker Canyon, where a small spring seeps from the canyon side. This canyon was named in 1936 after Monument employees had found the spring, and had seen on a rock near it names and dates scratched long ago among unintelligible Indian signs. One, "W.B.R., 1849," may have been made by W.B. Rude of the Jayhawkers. There is also a "rier" which may be the last part of the name Brier; the Brier family tagged on behind the Jayhawkers. The name of a man in Doctor French's party of 1860 was also found, and a few other names that have not been identified.

❖ The road dips across rolling country for about 2 miles to the Western Entrance of Death Valley National Monument, 56 m., in Towne's Pass, (alt. 5500), which was named in 1860 by Doctor Darwin French in honor of a member of the 1849 party.

Sec. c.   Western Monument Entrance to Lone Pine, 65 m., Calif. 190

West of Towne's Pass, Calif. 190 descends through a long canyon in the Panamint Range to Panamint Valley, and then circles the north end of the Slate Ranch. The tawny, widespread desert is quite arid and, except for the two small settlements of Darwin and Keeler, is almost uninhabited. The highway passes over rugged upland hills, with mountain ranges rising to the north and south, to the foot of the Sierra Nevada.

❖ West of the boundary of Death Valley National Monument, 0 m., the road descends through a steep canyon. Three water barrels along the way supply first aid for heated radiators; many cars boil coming up this grade, particularly in the afternooon when there is a following wind. At 7 mi. the Argus Range is visible toward the west, sweeping up from Panamint Valley. It is a mountain wall more than 6000 feet high; beyond its crests are the Inyo Mountains and the Sierra Nevada.

Panamint Valley (alt. 1614), with barren yellow-browns, is surrounded by stark mountains streaked with color; to the north huge sand dunes lie heaped at the foot of the range. The clay playa that fills the center of the flat valley is scored by a single straight road. In early spring beautiful flowers grow beside the route; the most abundant is Death Valley sunflower, a pretty, cosmos-like yellow bloom, with a dark center. Primroses and the pink Chinese lantern mallow, sometimes called fivespot because of the dark markings at the base of each of the five petals, are found here.

❖ Panamint Airfield (L), 10.4 m., cannot be used if wet.

❖ At 11.3 m. is a junction with the Wildrose Canyon-Trona Road (see Tour 7).

❖ Panamint Motel (alt. 2000) is at 14.2 m. (service station, garage, cabins, meals, camp sites, trailer camp).

By the motel is (L) a junction with the Zinc Hill Road (see Tour 10).

West of the motel Calif. 190 crosses Darwin Wash, surmounts a small saddle, enters a deep canyon with brightly colored walls, and climbs along the left wall to the head of the canyon. The route continues in a series of easy loops, rounds a shoulder of the mountains at 26.3 m., and crosses a valley toward the Coso Range.

❖ At 14.8 m. is a junction with a dirt road.

Right on this road, at 5.2 m., the buildings and reduction plant of the Darwin Lead Mine are visible on the mountain. (L).

Darwin (alt. 4749; pop 100), 6.2 m. (gas station, garage, store, meals) is on a mesa above Darwin Wash. The wash, named in 1860 by Doctor Darwin French, determined the name of the town that sprang up when lead and silver were discovered in 1875. At the peak of the boom, 1500 people were living here. Darwin has had several booms since then, but today not more than 75 houses are left in the old mining town, sitting silently in the sun. There is no water here; in 1875 a 12-mile pipe line was built to springs in the Coso Mountains (R), but when the pipe became old it leaked so much that no water reached town; water is now hauled from Darwin Falls, 8 miles away.

1. Right from Darwin 2 m. to an Indian Camp. The Shoshone here once lived on the other side of the wash, but they "had a sickness" and many of them died. To rid themselves of the spirits of the departed, who seemed to be bringing them evil, the survivors burned the village and settled where they are now.

2. Left from Darwin is a rough road over Lane Hill and Zinc Hill (see Tour 10), which loops back and meets Calif. 190 on the edge of Panamint Valley (see above).

Calif. 190 continues west, crossing the hills and descending through a rough and sandy terrain lying beneath low hills of dark purplish brown lava, to the grayish saline flats of Owens Lake. Before the city of Los Angeles bought the water of Owens Valley, a blue lake had sparkled here. In the 70s, silver bullion, cast in the form of small logs, was brought from the Cerro Gordo (Sp.: *big hill*) Mine, almost at the summit (alt. 9217) of Cerro Gordo Mountain (R), to be piled like cordwood on the shores of the lake. A little steamer ferried it across in 24 hours, saving a week-long haul in freight wagons. The silver was then shipped to San Francisco.

The Sierra Nevada rises grandly above Owens Valley, the serrated crests running in a long line against the western sky. The granite peaks thrust sharply upward, their almost perpendicular faces bare of the snow that lies below in high canyons and valley. Early in the morning the light from the sun rising over the Inyo Range (R) turns this snow rose-pink.

❖ Keeler (alt. 3610; pop. 100), 50 m. (gas, meals, and other facilities), is on the old shoreline of Owens Lake. For many years there has been a Soda Ashplant(L) here, engaged in extracting soda from the lake bed.

❖ At 63 m. is a junction with US 395.

Left here on US 395 to Mojave, 113 m.

Right at the junction with Calif. 190 on US 395.

❖ Lone Pine (alt. 3500; pop 300) 65m. (all accommodations), is a small town strung along the highway, which is Main Street. The town lies at the base of the Sierra Nevada. Center of a cluster of granite peaks reaching out toward the sky is Mount Whitney (alt. 14,495), the highest peak in the 48 States. Mount Langley (alt. 14,042), nearer to Lone Pine than Mount Whitney, is frequently mistaken for it.

Tour 2:

Junction with Calif. 190—Greenwater Valley—
Salsberry Pass—Junction with East Highway;
53 m.

Update:

❖ Roads termed "oiled roadbed" are paved.
❖ The road to Ryan is a private road with access restricted to residents only. The sightseeing train is no longer in operation.
❖ Use care along this route. Although cable netting has been installed over many old mining sites, several drop-offs remain.
❖ In addition to the remains of Greenwater, ruins of the former boomtowns at Furnace and Ramsey can be viewed on the route.
❖ The cabin at Greenwater Spring is no longer there.
❖ There is no water at Bradbury Well.

Oiled roadbed between Calif. 190 and Dante's View; rest graded dirt.

Dante's View, one of the most popular lookouts in Death Valley is reached by this route. The road also passes the early borax town of Ryan. On a short road is the site of Greenwater, an early mining town. As it continues south the road loops around the end of the Black Mountains to join the East Highway at Ashford Junction.

❖ This route branches southeast from Calif. 190 in Furnace Creek

Dante's View, a 6000-foot vantage point in the Black Mountains. On the valley floor are chalky salt beds and on the horizon Telescope Peak, the highest point in the Panamint Range.

Wash (see Tour 1, sec. b), 0 m., 1.5 miles west of the western boundary of the Monument. It runs up toward brilliant small hills that push through the surface of the wash. On the green and fawn sides of the Black Mountains (R) are jumbled patches of color; the mass is topped with the black lava that gives the range its name. In the dark flanks of the mountains behind Ryan is a section of mountain wall (L) with soft, delicate colors; the whole looks surprisingly like an enormous stage set of very modern design in the solitude of the desert.

❖ At 2.6 m. is a junction with an oiled road.

> Left on this road to Ryan (alt. 2500), 2 m., looking out over Furnace Creek Wash to Death Valley. Borax mines were operated here from 1914 to 1928; the houses for the employees were well built and the company even provided tennis courts. Borax was shipped out over a narrow-gauge railroad to a refinery at Death Valley Junction. The section of the railroad between Death Valley Junction and Ryan has been torn out but 7 miles of track between Ryan and the mines remain. Sight-seeing trains (fare $1, guide) are run on this route, which skirts the rim of the canyon and offers magnificent changing vistas of Death Valley.

The panorama of Dante's View is without peer anywhere in the world. From nearly 6000 feet above sea level, one may see the lowest point in Death Valley—a sheer drop of 282 feet below sea level near Badwater.

South of Ryan Junction, the road climbs the wash to Greenwater Valley (alt. 4000) in the Black Mountains. The air here is clear and sharp.

❖ At 7.9 m. is a junction with an oiled road.

Right on this road up the slope, through a steep, winding canyon to Dante's View (alt. 5220), 6 m., on the summit of the Black Mountains. (This should be visited in the morning when the light effects are best.) The viewpoint, more than a mile above the valley, is, in turn, a mile below the summit of Telescope, which is opposite. Westward over the Panamints, among the white crests of the distant Sierra, is Mount Whitney (alt. 14,495); just below is Badwater (279.6 feet below sea level). One sweep of the eyes encompasses the two extremes of land altitude in the 48 States.

The great mountain walls that baffled the early overland travelers stretch north and south, their sides torn by deep canyons; the Owlshead and the Avawatz Mountains are clearly visible (L) as Death Valley's southern barrier. Below in the Valley itself, which here is narrow, white salt areas are sharply outlined against brown and gray slopes; the green spots are

Bennett's and Mesquite Wells (L) and Furnace Creek Ranch (R). To the east also the view is dramatic. The Amargosa Desert stretches below the contorted foothills of the Black Mountains. In the foreground (L) is Forty-Mile Canyon, where the Briers burned their wagons in December, 1849 (see Early White Visitors). Barren, isolated ranges are eastward on the desert—the Bare, the Shoshone, and the Skull Mountains, the Spotted, the Pintwater and the Desert Ranges, solidly backed by the Charleston Range on the horizon.

The road now passes below patches (R) cleared on the slope; they show where the town of Greenwater (see below) once sprawled for 2 miles.

❖ At 12.7 m. is a junction with a dirt road.

Right here to the site of Greenwater, 1.9 m., now only a scattering of beer bottles, weatherworn boards, and a few stone foundations, amid the desert vegetation that is once more covering the slope. Gold and silver were found here in 1884, but the settlement did not become active until 1905, when copper was dis-

Tourists at Dante's View

covered. Greenwater then boomed after the manner of mining towns, and had a newspaper, banks and numerous saloons. Early automobiles snorted and jerked their way over the hills. Although everything, even water, had to be carried in, two or three thousand people lived here and combed the adjacent hills for prospects. One claim was registered as being in Cemetary Park, Funeral Range, Death Valley. The deposit of copper ore, though rich, was shallow, and Greenwater dwindled rapidly.

Right 2 m. from Greenwater on a rough road to Greenwater Spring (alt. 5000). The road ends in front of a small, unpainted cabin; the spring is at the end of a low tunnel, about 200 yards left, which was dug in an attempt to furnish the now dead camp with a water supply. The little cabin has a small room with a stove improvised from a galvanized iron washtub, a stall, a manger for burros, and, in the rear, a dugout cellar with a ventilating pipe.

Toward the east the Black Mountains slope down swiftly to a row of low hills. Beyond are the tan and rose desert and sun-burned mountain ranges of Nevada. When the big, soft desert clouds fill the sky, and their shadows drift over miles of flat country and mountain ranges, the changing light and color produce one of the most beautiful views to be found in the Death Valley region.

❖ South of the junction with the Greenwater Road is a junction, 15.6 m., with the Greenwater Canyon Road (See Tour 11) leading to Death Valley Junction.

❖ The road crosses the scarcely perceptible summit (alt. 4200), 20 m., and proceeds toward southern Death Valley.

❖ At 32.3 m. is a junction with Deadman's Pass Road, a very rough route leading to Death Valley Junction. Deadman's Pass Road received its name during the Greenwater boom days when the body of an unknown man was found there; along the road were also the bones of horses that had died under the strain of hauling freight up the grade.

❖ At 42 m. is a junction with a dirt road.

Left here to a junction with Calif. 127, 7 m., and to Shoshone, on Calif. 127, 8 m.

❖ The main route turns sharply right here, crosses a wide valley, and ascends an easy grade to Salsberry Pass (alt. 3000), 47.5 m., in the lower end of the Black Mountains.

❖ Bradbury Well (alt. 1545), 49 m., is boarded over; a bucket and a rope are used to obtain water. There are several small caves in the surrounding hills.

West of Bradbury Well the road passes between grotesque, bright-colored formations. Butte Valley (see Tour 14), with the striped butte that gave it its name, is visible westward across Death Valley.

❖ Jubilee Pass, 53.2m., just north of Jubilee Mountain (alt. 2511), offers an easy entrance into Death Valley. To the north and the west are excellent views of the Panamints, and of the low dip of Wingate Wash.

❖ The East Highway (see Tour 3) is reached at 53 m., 2 miles southeast of Ashford Junction.

Tour 3:

Furnace Creek Junction—Badwater—Ashford
Junction—Saratoga Springs Junction
63 m. on East Highway

Update:

❖ Roads termed "oiled roadbed" are paved.

❖ Self-guided tour pamphlets are available for purchase at the side of the road just south of Furnace Creek Junction.

❖ Golden Canyon is now accessible to hikers only; the road washed out some time ago; pieces of the old parking lot can still be seen.

❖ Due to erosion, and perhaps some vandalism, Mushroom Rock looks less like a vegetable today; some say it more closely resembles "E.T."

❖ Volcanic Drive is now called Artist's Drive.

❖ The dirt road to Devil's Golf Course, the Salt Pools and Natural Bridge are all good dirt roads.

❖ Cars must be parked about three-quarters of a mile from Natural Bridge. It is accessible from there only on foot.

❖ The road south of Confidence Mill is recommended for 4WD only.

❖ The elevation of Rogers Peak is 9994; what is called Manly Peak in the text is now named Bennett Peak, elevation 9980.

Oiled roadbed between Furnace Creek Junction and Ashford Junction; remainder, graded dirt.

This road, known as the East Highway, explores the eastern side and southern end of Death Valley, running below the brilliantly colored flanks of the Black Mountains and along the Salt Beds, and passing the lowest point in North America. Several side routes lead into canyons.

❖ Branching south from Calif. 190 at Furnace Creek Junction, 0 m. (See Tour 1, sec. b), the East Highway runs along the base of the Black Mountains at sea level. Gold-colored hills lie below soft red mountains (L); the tall peak in the Panamints (R) is Telescope, whose tip is more than 2 miles above Death Valley. Immediately north of Telescope are Manly Peak (alt. 10,000) and Rogers Peak (alt. 9000), named for the two saviors of the Death Valley immigrant party.

❖ At 2.1 m. is a junction with a dirt road.

> Left on this road through Golden Canyon, whose rose and terracotta walls curve up through brilliantly painted hills, to the end of an automobile road, 1 m.; from this point a short trail leads to a pillared Amphitheatre spectacularly colored.

❖ Mushroom Rock, 4.6 m., an oddly shaped lava formation, has been carved by wind-driven sand into the semblance of the floret of a gigantic cauliflower.

❖ At 5 m. is a junction with an unpaved one-way road, looping back to the main road.

Golden Canyon

Mushroom Rock

Left on this road to Volcanic Drive, 0.2 m., which winds upward through hills, first of brown lava, then of yellow clay, tinted with rose, with a strange milky green, and with warm tans and browns. At the summit the colored strata tilt toward the sky.

Descending through yellow walls, the road turns sharply at 3.3 m., becoming Artists' Drive, and climbs again between yellow chalky cliffs.

At 4.7 m., is a junction with a dirt road, left here, 0.2 m., to Kaleidoscope View. The cliff for which the spot is named is green, rose, and tan; it looks as if a child had used it as a palette.

The main side road passes bright, yet soft-colored, hills, and crosses a cinder-covered slope, where the lower end of Death Valley comes into view. Its floor is covered with wandering streaks of white, soft purple, and brown; the Panamints (R) dwindle toward the Owlshead Mountains. The low gap between the ranges is Wingate Pass. The road descends through low tan and brown hills, and enters the enfilades of a narrow-walled canyon, to reach the main road at 9 m.

West of the entrance to Volcanic Drive and below the highway (R) is the Devil's Golf Course, so named because only a fiend could play the

Devil's Golf Course (inset: salt "cupola")

game on its extraordinary surface. Ridges and pinnacles of crystallized salt rise 2 to 12 inches, with here and there specimens 3 feet high. They break under a trampling boot with a ringing sound.

❖ At 6.3 m. is a junction with the West Highway (see Tour 4), which rejoins the East Highway at Ashford Junction (see below).

❖ At 11.3 m. is a junction with a dirt road.

> Right here across the Salt Beds to the Salt Pools, 0.5 m., whose translucent water is so saturated that crystals constantly form on the surface. They drift to the side of the pool, or sink and become part of the Salt Beds. The salt forms so rapidly that the pools must be blasted each year.

At 13.3 m. is a junction with a dirt road (restricted to use of cars of less than 190-inch overall measurement).

> Left here to Natural Bridge, 1.7 m., an imposing rock span, 50 feet long and 55 feet high, joining the sides of the canyon.

❖ Badwater (279.6 feet below sea level), 16.8 m., is the lowest point in North America. A marker has been placed on the mountain (E) to show the ocean level. The pools of Badwater, in the rough, tan-colored

Badwater. Supt. Leik of Mt. McKinley, first man to stand on both the top and bottom of North America, March 1939.

surface of the Salt Beds, were named in the early days by someone who found the water very bad, indeed, as it still is. More than a mile above is Dante's View (see Tour 2) on the edge of the Black Mountains.

South of Badwater the road curves around the spurs of the varicolored mountains. Their strata are bent and twisted; here and there are large patches of solid color—soft yellow, a weathered yet vivid pink, rose, lavender, and vermilion. The detrital fans of the Black Mountains, negligible in comparison with those of the Panamints, have been called wineglass fans. The small fan is the base, the vertical canyon walls are the stem, and the slopes above the narrow canyon, worn away before the canyon was uplifted by faulting, are the bowl of the glass.

❖ Mormon Point, 33 m., a huge mass of red, brown, and black, is supposed to have been named for Mormons who were mining here in the 1860s. The Mormons were indefatigable travelers in the Southwest, but their detailed records contain no mention of Mormons in Death Valley during the early days.

❖ The Ruins of Ashford Mill (R), 44 m., top a small rise. This custom mill was built in 1914 when the Ashford Mine, in a canyon (L), and the Carbonate Mine, in the Death Valley side of the Panamints, were producing. There was not enough ore, however, to keep it running, and it fell into decay.

Custom milling—milling other people's ore—is a delicate business. Rarely does any miner receive what he believes to be the value of his ore; he views the prosperity of the owner of the mill with dark suspicion.

❖ At 45 m. is Ashford Junction. Right is the junction with the West Highway (see Tour 4).

The East Highway now rises over gently rounded mesas.

❖ At 47 m. is the junction (L) with the Salsberry Pass road (see Tour 2).

❖ Little of the Confidence Mill (17 feet below sea level), 48 m. built in the early days, is left but a pit.

South of Confidence Mill the road skirts a dry lake bed, or playa (L). When wet this playa is slippery and soft, and churned paths through the center show where cars have found the going difficult. Damp spots on playas are dangerous and should be avoided. The road continues southeast over the great fan from the Owlshead Mountains (R) and the Avawatz Mountains. The beauty of lower Death Valley is less somber than that of the upper valley. The clear blue desert sky spreads widely; the mountains are lower, and there are great stretches of light, sandy wash.

❖ At 53 m. is a junction (R) with a rough dirt road (see Tour 12).

❖ Saratoga Springs Junction is at 63 m.

Left from the junction 2 m. on a rough road to Saratoga Springs (primitive bathouse), pools amid swampy marshes with a thick growth of grass and rushes. This is another home of the tiny Death Valley fish; and in the winter many kinds of waterfowl are here—some permanent inhabitants, some migrants, and some wintering.

When the Baily Geological Party camped here on Christmas Day 1900, someone put up a sign that said in part:

20 Miles from Wood
20 Miles from Water
40 Feet from Hell
God Bless our Home!

South of Saratoga Springs Junction a rough road continues 28 miles through the extreme southeastern corner of Death Valley Monument to a junction with Calif. 127, about 30 miles north of Baker on U.S. 466.

Tour 4:

Junction with East Highway—Salt Beds—Shorty's
Grave—Ashford Junction

39 m. West Highway

Update:

- ❖ The West Highway is now called West Side Highway. It is a good, graded road; the East Highway is paved.
- ❖ Shorty's Well and Gravel Well are dry.
- ❖ At the Eagle Borax Works site are a parking lot, marker and chemical toilet.

Graded dirt road.

The West Highway, on higher ground, parallels the old dusty road used by the 20-mule borax teams. Side routes lead from it to canyons of the Panamints. The road rejoins the East Highway at Ashford Junction.

❖ The West Highway branches southwest from the East Highway (see Tour 3), 0 m., at a point 6.3 m. south of Furnace Creek Junction, and crosses the Salt Beds. An occasional, pure-white channel of salt shows in the rough dusty crust, which is very hard and rings when kicked or broken. In some places the crust can be broken through to an oozy mess below. Parts of the Salt Beds are marshy, with small streams. The early road, used by the 20-mule teams, was beaten flat with sledge-hammers. It ran down the dusty center of the Valley.

❖ An Iron Casing (R), 2.3 m., is one of several that were driven through 1250 feet of alternate layers of clay and salt, without reaching the bedrock of Death Valley. It is believed that each layer indicates a drying up of the old lake bed.

❖ West of the Salt Beds the road crosses a small clay flat. The Valley widens at 6.5 m., and the road traverses a sandy, stony plain lying on the lower edge of the detrital fans from the Panamints. The Owlshead Mountains, across Death Valley's southern end, are barren, having neither water nor grass.

❖ At 10.4 m. is a junction with a dirt road.

Left on this road to Tule Spring, 0.3 m., a small waterhole.

❖ At 11.3 m. is a junction (R) with the Hanaupah Canyon Road (see Tour 13), and with a short dirt road.

Left here 200 feet is Shorty's Well, roofed over to protect the good water and equipped with a pump.

❖ A monument at 13 m., built of local stone by the Park Service in 1936, stands between the Graves of Shorty Harris and Jim Dayton. The bronze plaque on the monument says:

Bury me beside Jim Dayton in the Valley we loved; Above me write: "Here lies Shorty Harris, a single-blanket prospector." Epitaph requested by Shorty (Frank) Harris, beloved gold hunter. 1856-1934.

Here lies Jas. Dayton, pioneer, perished 1898.

To these trailmakers, whose courage matched the dangers of the land, this bit of earth is dedicated forever.

Shorty was a very short, chunky man, with shiny gold caps over his front teeth. He was a familiar figure to many as he stumped along with his burros, covering the whole Death Valley region on foot. Although he worked many claims, he never made much money. His two most famous strikes were Rhyolite (see Tour 5) and Harrisburg (see Tour 7).

James Dayton came to Death Valley in the 1880s, and drove one of the first 20-mule teams. He was called Sailor, though his seafaring experience was acquired when he was a cook on a Sacramento River boat. When borax was no longer teamed out of Death Valley, he

Monument to Shorty Harris and Jim Dayton

became the caretaker at Furnace Creek Ranch. Whenever supplies ran low, he hitched four horses to a wagon and drove 140 miles to Daggett for more. He was 62 when, in July of 1898, he started out on his final trip. A searching party sent out when he did not appear at Daggett found his body here beside the wagon, guarded by his dog, who was so weak he could hardly drag himself about. He had been able to get water, but the horses, which had been tied to the wagon wheels, had died of thirst. The searchers buried Dayton here; for many years the bleached bones of his horses lay on the grave, which was further marked by an ironing board on which his name had been etched with a hot poker.

❖ At 13.5 m. is a junction with a dirt road.

Left on this road to the Eagle Borax Works (250 feet below sea level), 0.2 m. This little plant, the first to extract borax in Death Valley, was built in 1880 by Isidore Daunet, but it was operated for only a few months. When the rumor that Aaron Winters had found borax in Death Valley (see Borax) sped through the desert settlements, Daunet remembered what he had seen on a trip in the Valley during the summer of 1875. With six other men he had left the dying camp of Panamint City (see Tour 19) bound for the mines of Arizona; the party started to take a short cut through Death Valley. Their water was soon gone, however, and the heat-crazed men cut the throats of their burros and gulped the blood. Daunet and one other man retraced their wavering tracks to a spring by a marsh where some Indians were camping. The Indians rescued two more of the party, but the intense heat and thirst had been too much for the rest. It was the marsh by the spring that Daunet remembered, and he filed a mineral claim to 260 acres of it. Then he and his partners bought an iron vat in Daggett, together with some 1000-gallon pans that have long since vanished, and hauled the unwieldy objects here over 140 miles of almost roadless desert. The borax they recovered from the marsh was impure and only a few tons were sold; the venture was soon abandoned. The pile of borax beside the road has been lying here since Daunet and his partners left.

A herd of handsome wild burros grazes on the luxuriant marsh grasses; their scrubby, woolly parents or grandparents

Burros were valuable to the 1850s desert prospectors because they drank little water and could carry loads almost twice their weight. Today their increasing numbers threaten the native bighorn sheep.

carried packs over these hills. They have reverted in type to the sleek ass that was brought to the Americas by the Spaniards.

❖ At 17 m. is a junction with a dirt road.

Left on this road to Bennett's Well (266 feet below sea level), 0.3 m. here in the grove of shrubby mesquite, Charles Bennett of Pahrump had a rest camp and watering station for his mules during the year he freighted borax for the Harmony Works. The borax company continued to use it, but the windmill they installed to give a plentiful supply of water now turns aimlessly in the breeze.

In 1849, while Manly and Rogers were hunting a road to civilization for the Bennett-Arcane party (see First White Visitors), the rest of the party waited at a spring south of Furnace Creek. For many years it was believed that they had camped here, but this is unlikely. Manly says that there was no shade at the camp—the travelers had to sit under their wagons to find shelter from the sun—and the mesquite at Bennett's Well has a considerable height now, as it must have had in 1849. It is probable that the camp site was by the open water where the Eagle Borax Works now are, or at Tule Spring.

In 1860 Doctor Darwin French found toys and castaway clothing at a spot which he decided must have been the camp of 1849, and he called it Bennett's Holes for Asa Bennett. But it is not known whether that particular Bennett's Holes was here, for more than 20 years later, when another Bennett came to Death Valley, he watered his mules and had a camp at this place, which has ever since been called Bennett's Well.

❖ Gravel Well (R), 22.7 m., beside the road, has good sweet water.

In the center of the Valley is the Abandoned Mesquite Well (244 feet below sea level) in a grove of shrubby mesquite. This was an important station on the 20-mule-team route to Mojave, with the last good water on the route in Death Valley. Pack rats quickly discovered the barley stored to feed the mules, and an enormous colony settled in the grove, building untidy nests of heaped sticks and brush. Drivers and swampers who forgot their presence and left small articles lying around when they went to sleep often failed to find them in the morning; but they were never in doubt about the cause of the disappearance, because the rats always left a stick or a pebble in honest exchange for what they had taken.

❖ At 31 m. is a junction with a road to Warm Spring, Butte Valley, Anvil Springs, Greater View, and Goler Wash. (see Tour 14).

❖ The Grave of an Unknown, 32.4 m., is marked with crude corner posts and a heap of stones. Death Valley Scotty, who on one of his lone trips in the Valley found what was left of the body, dug the grave.

❖ At 34.4 m. is a junction with the Wingate Pass Road (see Tour 15).

❖ Shoreline Butte (R), 35.5 m., is a mass of black basalt rising 600 feet from the Valley floor. Its terraced sides—about six terraces are easily distinguishable—were worn by water when Death Valley was a lake. This probably occurred at the end of the last glacial period, when the rains were constant and heavy, and the Amargosa River roared down through Nevada to pour into the lower end of the lake here; Owens Lake, at the base of the Sierra Nevada, flooded Searles Lake and Panamint Valley.

In the lower end of Death Valley, the Black Mountains (L) are vivid with light brick-red patches, and on the slope at their feet are several small black basalt buttes, shaped like whales.

❖ At Ashford Junction, 39 m., the West Highway joins the East Highway (see Tour 3).

Tour 5:

Beatty Junction—Hell's Gate—Daylight Pass—
Rhyolite, Nev.

26.8 m. The Beatty Road

Update:

❖ The route from Beatty Junction to Rhyolite is all paved.
Today it's known as "Daylight Pass Cutoff." Daylight Pass has
been extended from Rhyolite to Hwy. 190.

❖ The road to the Keane Wonder Mine is dusty, but good,
graded dirt.

❖ No water is available at Hole in the Rock Spring, or at Keane
Spring.

❖ The road to Keane Spring is recommended for 4WD vehicles
only.

❖ The Daylight Spring Ranger Station is now located at Beatty.

❖ Respect all private property, and no trespassing signs. The
Rhyolite area is still mined today. The Bottle House at Rhyolite still stands, but it is no longer a commercial establishment. Nearby mining activity threatens the remaining structures, prompting the formation of a grass-roots organization,
Friends of Rhyolite, to save the historical ruins (see Appendix).

Oiled roadbed between Beatty Junction and Monument Boundary,
remainder graded dirt.

The Beatty Road climbs the Funeral Mountains to Daylight Pass,
which is between the Funerals and the Grapevines. East of the Monu-

Ruins are all that are left of the Keane Wonder Mine. Gold was found at the mine in 1903 and in 1907 it produced some 1,800 tons a month.

ment it traverses the upland Amargosa Desert to Rhyolite, one of the famous ghost towns of the area.

❖ The Beatty Road branches northeast from Calif. 190, 0 m. (see Tour 1, sec. b), climbing the Valley wall diagonally through oddly colored round hills. Gay varicolored strata and splotches of solid color enliven the Funerals (R).

❖ At 6 m. is a junction with a rough dirt road.

> Right on this road to the Keane Wonder Mine Refinery (alt. 3000), 5.3 m., built after a gold discovery of 1903. Only a few buildings and the stamp mill are left; the desert wind whistles through the ruins. The mine was farther up the canyon, and buckets swinging on an overhead line carried the ore down to this place.

The road ascends the alluvial fan of Boundary Canyon, heading toward the dark Death Valley Buttes. Hills protrude from the surface of the fan that is gradually rising around them.

❖ Hell's Gate (alt. 2263), 10.5 m., was named in 1905 when teams leaving the protecting walls of the canyon would start and shake their heads as the burning summer heat scorched their tender noses. "They thought they had stuck their noses through the gates of hell," one teamster said. Hell's Gate is one of the most accessible of the several viewpoints on the rim of Death Valley. Below, toward the south, brown, mauve, and white streaks converge on the Salt Beds. The Funerals (L) curve toward Furnace Creek Wash, and the Panamints (R) culminate in the sharp point of Telescope Peak. From Hell's Gate are clearly seen the length and height of the huge alluvial fans, some of which rise 2000 feet. The setting sun paints the mountains with brilliant colors and fills the deep canyons with shadows.

East of Hell's Gate the grade is steep, and the low walls of Boundary Canyon—between the Grapevines and the Funerals—draw closer together. Left the broad red and gray bandings of Corkscrew Peak (alt. 5000) wind to a small, flat top. In the spring Boundary Canyon has a beautiful display of flowers. The wash is stippled with blue when the lovely indigo bush blooms; it has deep blue, pea-shaped flowers above dark green tiny leaves set on bone-white twigs. In vivid contrast with the blue is the flame pink of the mallow.

❖ At 11.8 m. is a junction with a foot trail.

> Left on this trail to Hole in the Rock Spring (alt. 3127), 0.3 m.

where a quart or so of water collects in a basin—enough to give a man or a burro a drink.

❖ At 14.2 m. is a junction with a rough road.

Right up this canyon to Keane Spring, 2 m. There is little water here, although at one time it provided the water supply for Chloride City (see Tour 17).

❖ On the summit of Daylight Pass (alt. 4,317), 17 m., is a Ranger Checking Station (see General Information).

Left from the ranger station to Daylight Spring, 0.3 m. This formerly pleasant camping place was first called Delightful Spring, but bearded prospectors shortened the name to Delight, and then changed it to Daylight, possibly because it catches the early sun. Today the water is piped to the ranger station.

❖ The boundary of the Monument—also the State Line between California and Nevada—is reached at 17.5 m.; in Nevada the road runs down to the Amargosa Desert, 18 m., a high, wide plain covered with desert brush.

❖ At 23 m. is a junction (L) with the Leadfield-Titus Canyon Road (see Tour 16).

❖ At 23 m. is a junction with the Chloride City-Chloride Cliff Road (see Tour 17).

The Beatty Road crosses the Amargosa Desert toward the pointed Bullfrog Hills, their jagged strata sloping toward the broad plain.

Right is Bare Mountain (alt. 6235), splotched with rose-red and creamy white outcrops and with spectacular vertical strata. South are the sand dunes near Death Valley Junction.

❖ The Site of Bullfrog is at 26 m.; the place was named for the mine found by Shorty Harrris and Ed Cross in 1904, when they camped here on their way to the new gold field at Tonopah. Shorty is credited with the discovery, the most famous of several he made. He selected the name because, as he said, the first piece of green rock he found "looked like a fat bullfrog sitting on my hand."

As soon as he reached Tonopah, Shorty sold out for $800, but Ed Cross held on and received $60,000 for his half-share. The original Bullfrog Mine was on the Edge of the Bullfrog Hills, 3 miles north.

Soon after the discovery, the space along the slope at the foot of the hills was dotted with tents; the clump nearest the mine was named Amargosa, and the little settlement between Amargosa and Bullfrog was called Jumpertown—its inhabitants were continually jumping back and forth between Amargosa and Bullfrog. A few hundred yards from the road are (L) the white stone walls of the old two-room jail. Roof and doors are gone, but the bars in the two window openings remain solidly in place.

❖ Rhyolite, Nevada (alt. 3600; pop 3), 26.8 m., has been the prize ghost town of the Southwest for many years; at one period it had a population of 12,000. Bullfrog was not sufficiently commodious and elegant for the taste of its settlers, so they laid out an ambitous townsite on this slope. The bare strips in the desert, reaching almost to the mine dumps in the encircling hills, are its former streets. In an incredibly short space of time a full-fledged town sprang up, with a three-story hotel, two-story concrete buildings to house banks and the school, an elaborate railroad station, and stores and dwelling houses. Along the two principal streets were chiefly saloons and gambling houses. Not all the inhabitants were miners, however; although the ore was rich, most of Rhyolite's money came from the sale of mining stock, issues of which were snatched up as fast as the certificates came off the presses.

Rhyolite was gay as only a mining town can be gay; money was plentiful and circulated freely. The town seldom went to bed; gambling and drinking places were jammed day and night. Men threw their money on the table of the Combination, the Sixty-Six, and the Louvre—which was run by a woman. Liquor must have been of doubtful quality; a man who sold his mine for $9000 publicly expressed his doubt that he would live to spend it because of the kind of whisky available.

After $3,000,000 had been taken from the mines, and while stock issues were selling fast, the panic of 1907 arrived. The flow of money to Rhyolite stopped almost overnight. In addition, the deposits of rich ore were already nearly exhausted. At the end of one short year the town stood deserted; most of the movable property of value had been taken out, even entire frame houses. The frame buildings that were left soon fell apart in the dry air; of hundreds of adobes, soon nothing was

The Bottle House in Rhyolite, circa 1930

left but walls sticking up here and there. Today even ghost Rhyolite is rapidly vanishing.

The Bottle House (R) was built mostly of beer bottles laid in clay. The house is decorated with bits of scrollwork and the painted wooden chimney still pretends to be of brick. Its owner operates the Bottle House as a museum (no charge, hours irregular) and sells bottles, arrowheads, bits of ore, and odds and ends picked up around the town as desert souvenirs. His garden contains cactus plants surrounded by brilliant patches of green, blue, and purple glass.

On the main street clean gray concrete walls rise starkly from a confusion of wreckage; everything usable has been removed and only squares of calcimine show where rooms were. A thick-walled Strongroom in one building shows signs of having been used by campers; slabs of concrete make a small corral beside it. Two or three houses on the slope (L) are sometimes occupied.

The Shoshone Mine (R) was found by the Indian, Shoshone Johnny; he sold the mine to Bob Montgomery for a new pair of overalls and a team of mules and drove proudly away to his home in Death Valley. The Shoshone brought the new owner much more than a pair of overalls and a team of mules.

Past grandeur has its sole representative in the Railroad Station at the upper end of the main street. There is no longer any railroad, but this gabled structure was so solidly built that it looks much as it did in 1907. It was used in 1938 to house a casino, with bar and dance hall. The railroad tracks have been torn up, the ties sold for firewood, and the right-of-way of the former railroad is now a road running to Beatty, on Nev. 5. It is a rather blood-curdling route, for its washboard surface leads through narrow cuts and the fills seem hardly wide enough. A new road between Beatty and Death Valley will circle the Bullfrog Hills (R).

Tour 6:

Junction with Calif. 190—Ubehebe Crater; *38.5 m.*

Update:

❖ The route from the Junction with Calif. 190 to Ubehebe Crater is good, paved road.

❖ There is no water at the Stove Pipe Wells handpump.

❖ The remains of the Bottle-House Dugout are now gone.

❖ There is no water at Triangle Springs.

❖ The Park Service has installed two interpretive displays along this stretch of Calif. 190: one explains the wagon wheel roads near the Sand Dune area, the other interprets the massive merging alluvial fans of the Panamints and Grapevine mountains.

❖ The road to Mesquite Spring is paved; there is a campground at road's end.

❖ Guests are no longer housed at Scotty's Castle, but "living history" tours conducted by characters from the 1930s are scheduled regularly throughout the day. Expect some long waits during peak season; while you wait your turn explore the grounds using the inexpensive tour brochures, and take the Windy Point trail up to Scotty's grave.

❖ The Grapevine Canyon Road is now paved.

❖ The end of the road to Ubehebe Canyon is a paved, one-way loop.

Oiled roadbed for 33.5 miles; balance, graded dirt.

This highway traverses northern Death Valley, passing the sandy wastes of what was once Lost Valley. A side route in Grapevine Canyon leads to one of the show places of Death Valley—Scotty's Castle. The main route ends at Ubehebe Crater, cradled in cinder hills, a relic of the Valley's prehistoric days.

❖ This road branches north from Calif. 190, 0 m., 18.4 miles north of Furnace Creek Junction (see Tour 1, sec. b). The junction is at the foot of the alluvial fan from Boundary Canyon. The road crosses the fan, going toward Strawberry Buttes, whose soft pink is dun in the early morning light. The stones on the fan are of many colors, coming as they do from the varicolored mountains, but from a distance they blend into the grayish tone characteristic of all the detrital fans.

❖ At 2.8 m. is a junction with a dirt road.

> Left on this road to the Grave of Val Nolan (R), 0.3 m., marked by a loose heap of stones and a sand-etched headboard. He died here "about Aug. 6, 1931. Buried, Nov. 6, 1931."
>
> Stove Pipe Wells (4.9 feet below sea level), 0.4 m., is now covered; an old-fashioned hand pump stands on the flat rock and cement top. The water is good, though slightly brackish. The wells, merely holes in the sand dug by a prospector years ago, saved many lives when they furnished the only water on the road that crossed Death Valley here. Because the winds often refilled

Remains of the Bottle House Dugout, Stovepipe Wells, 1935

the holes with sand, hiding the "wells" completely, someone finally stuck up a few lengths of rusty stovepipe to mark the spot; hence the name. The old stovepipe is now at Stove Pipe Wells Hotel (see Tour 1, sec. b).

Opposite are the rapidly disappearing remains of the Bottle-House Dugout, whose low walls were made of bottles laid in clay. In the early 1900s, the boom days of Death Valley, the freight road between Rhyolite and Skidoo crossed the Valley at this point; an enterprising business man established a primitive refreshment stand here, burying his beer in the sand to keep it cool. While the boom lasted he did a profitable business. In recent years the dugout has sheltered only an occasional traveler.

Left here 1.6 m. to a Wooden Cross in the Sand Dunes, where services are held in each year on Easter Sunday, as the sun rolls up over the Funerals and floods the dunes with light.

In the striped and folded red and black flanks of the Grapevines (R) is Thimble Peak (alt. 6000). On the other side of Death Valley (L) is the broad slope of Emigrant Wash. (It has long been a Western convention to call all early settlers who came overland "emigrants," rather than immigrants—a term reserved for application to people from abroad.)

❖ At 7.8 m. is a junction with a dirt road.

Left on this road to Triangle Springs, 1.4 m., at sea level, where there is good water and a pleasant camp site.

❖ At 15.4 m. is the junction with the exit road from Titus Canyon (see Tour 16).

❖ The road climbs gradually, and at about 24 m. (alt. 1000) the alluvial fans from the Panamints and the Grapevines merge. The desert brush is more verdant and grows more thickly here; there are many small barrel, flat-leaved, and cylindrical cactuses; in the spring the ground between them is thickly sprinkled with yellow, orange, white, and blue and lavender flowers.

❖ The road crosses the gullies of a wash at 30 m., dipping and rising like the track of a roller coaster. From the summit the northern part of Death Valley is visible; the mountain ranges on the sides draw together to pinch out the Valley. Imposing Tin Mountain (alt. 8900) is the end

Unloading household goods at Scotty's Castle; Albert Johnson by van, May 1930

of the Panamint Range (L). Although numerous mineral claims have been established on this mountain, no mines have been developed. The Grapevine Mountains (R) are taller at this end of the range; trees grow on Wahguhye Peak (alt. 8590) and Grapevine Peak (alt. 8705).

❖ At 33.5 m (alt 2500) is a junction with a dirt road.

> Left on this road to Mesquite Spring (alt. 1739), 1.5 m., is a sturdy growth of mesquite.

❖ At 33.5 m on the main road is a junction with a dirt road.

> Right on this road, which goes up through Grapevine Canyon. At 1 m. are 8-foot concrete fence posts that mark the boundary of the ranch belonging to the almost legendary Walter Scott, better known as Death Valley Scotty, and Albert M. Johnson.

> Huge doors (L) at 3 m., on a bridge, are the only entrance to Scotty's Castle (open 8-6; adm. $1), which is on a sheltered northern shelf of Grapevine Canyon. The style of the buildings is for the most part a free adaptation of the Provincial Spanish, with warm-toned walls and roofs in dusty red. On its way up to the court, the road runs by the unfinished swimming pool. The great main structure consists of two units connected by walls enclosing

a patio. Both units have towers, each of which has a wrought-iron weather vane that represents Scotty punching burros over a trail. There is a clock tower (L) beyond the house. A yard (R), on which Scotty's cabin once stood, is now surrounded by a long, low, verandaed guest house, the sheds and stables, the workers' quarters, and the workshops, all built of concrete; the yard is shaded by old fig and plum trees.

The main house has a two-story living-room, with a fireplace at one end and a fountain at the other. On the second floor is a balcony giving a wide view. The houses are embellished with imported tiling; men were brought over from Austria to carve the great doors and woodwork. The rear unit has a large garage, and huge freezing and cooling rooms. There are living quarters on the ground floor also, and above them many bedrooms having gay tiled bathrooms. The guest house is divided into suites, some of which have kitchens. Many of the fine old furnishings were brought from Spain, and those made in this country are harmonious in style. The water from Grapevine Springs is used to generate electricity. It has been asserted by the owners that the

Death Valley Scotty (left) and Albert Johnson

Interior of Scotty's Castle

showy castle cost them $2,000,000—which is not a fantastic sum, considering the difficulties of transportation and the five years consumed in construction, which is still uncompleted. The "swimming pool" is only a raw gash in the earth, and the buildings have lost some of their freshness. The 45-foot palms transplanted from San Bernardino have died and their feather-duster tops are now straw-colored.

For many years Death Valley Scotty has been a popular mystery. A blue-eyed, burly man, an ex-performer with Buffalo Bill, he would come storming out of Death Valley, shower Los Angeles with $100 bills, and disappear again. In 1905 he hurtled by special train from Los Angeles to Chicago in 45 hours, with great publicity. He often boasted of his hidden gold mines; but although the Death Valley region has been much explored his mines have never been found. Now that Scotty is becoming older, he spends most of his time secluded in his lower ranch on the borders of Death Valley, or lingering in desert towns.

The Grapevine Canyon Road continues through the completely vanished town of Bonnie Clare to a junction with Nev. 5 at about 20 m.; right here to Beatty; right at Beatty to Rhyolite (see Tour 5) for a loop route back to Death Valley.

Ubehebe Crater

North of the junction with Grapevine Canyon Road, the main highway drops down a little hill; the road in this end of the Valley is rather rough.

❖ At 34 m. is a junction with a dirt road.

Right on this road to a Spring, 0.5 m. The brown house half hidden in the trees (L) belongs to Scotty's Lower Ranch (not open to public).

A few yards farther a little stream, a foot wide, crosses the road; it comes from Scotty's ranch, where there are several springs on the bench (R) above the house.

❖ At 35.4 m. the road turns west to cross the Valley. Dry Mountain (alt. 8726), in the Last Chance Range, is ahead, with striking horizontal strata; dark patches, like cloud shadows, mark its flanks.

❖ At 35.8 m. is a junction with the Sand Springs Road (see Tour 18).

West of the junction the road becomes a one-way loop, passing between low, eroded mud cliffs to curl upward around the cinder hills.

❖ A short, sharp ascent ends at the edge of the Ubehebe (Ind.: *big basket in the rock*) Crater (alt. 2900), 38.5 m., facing a startlingly brilliant east wall where horizontal layers of red and orange are framed by pale gray and ocher slopes. Ubehebe Crater is an inverted cone, half a mile in diameter at the top, 800 feet deep, and 450 feet in diameter at the bottom. This is an explosion pit, or explosion crater, that did not build a large cone; there are several smaller craters of the same kind in the vicinity. The volcanic action probably occurred within the last 1000 years.

From the edge of the crater the road slips down a narrow hogback and skirts the left side, where a foot trail leads to a point offering a closer view. The road descends and then passes through mud bluffs, rejoining the main highway a few yards south of the point of departure.

Tour 7:
Emigrant Wash Ranger Station—Wildrose
Canyon—Ballarat

44.1 m. Emigrant Canyon Road

Update:

❖ The road to the Charcoal Kilns is paved, except for the final two miles which are a mixture of dirt and gravel. From that point of the tour on, 4WD is recommended; no buses, campers or trailers longer than 27 feet.

❖ "Auguerreberry" is usually spelled "Auguereberry" today.

❖ The Cyanide Mill is also known as Journigan's Mill.

❖ The houses at Skidoo are now gone; the old mill is extremely dangerous—do not venture into it.

❖ Heed the signs along Emigrant Pass and drive with great care.

❖ The former Summer Headquarters is now gone, but there is a campground at Wildrose.

❖ Right from Mahogany Flats is actually Rogers Peak, elevation 9994 feet, named for named for Manly's partner, John H. Rogers. Bennett's Peak, elevation 9980 feet, is located just south of Rogers. Manly Peak, elevation 7197 feet, is several miles south, outside the park's boundary.

❖ Telescope Peak measures 11,049 feet.

❖ The only facilities just south of Wildrose are picnic tables and a chemical toilet; no gas, meals or grocery store.

❖ The road to Trona is paved, but may not be maintained, especially following storms.

❖ Panamint George is long gone, but there are some residents still living in the Indian Ranch area. Respect private property.
❖ Chris Wicht's camp has been reduced to ruins.
❖ The Hearst's Minietta mine is no longer worked, but there is extensive mining activity near Ballarat. Use great caution in the area.

Oiled roadbed between ranger station and Monument boundary; side roads graded dirt.

This route climbs into the high Panamints, and its side routes to the ghost town of Skidoo and to Auguerreberry Point. In Wildrose Canyon a side route climbs to the timberline and then on up to a point more than 8000 feet above Death Valley. The main route continues down Wildrose Canyon through sun-baked Panamint Valley, to the ghost town of Ballarat.
❖ Emigrant Canyon Road branches south from Calif. 190 at Emigrant Wash Junction (alt. 1542) (see Tour 1, sec. b), 0 m.; 7.7 miles north of Towne Pass.
❖ Just inside the narrow entrance of Emigrant Canyon, 1.8 m., where the canyon broadens, the red sandstone wall (L) has been pillared by wind and water. The road runs up the wash, which has rounded hills on both sides. Desert shrubs and cactus are scattered over the wash and the slopes. A great variety of flowers decorates the canyon in April and May, among them sweet-scented golden and brown-eyed evening primroses, and blue, lavender, and purple desert heliotrope.
❖ Emigrant Spring (R) (alt. 4045), 4.8 m., is marked by a thick growth of green in a little basin above the road. For many years a horse trough stood here, filled with crystal-clear water fed from a rusty pipe. Burros and horses drank from the trough, and many a prospector has held his canteen to the pipe. This was a favorite camping place; smoke often wavered upward here while coffee was being boiled and bacon fried over a little rock fireplace.

The springs are now covered, and a standpipe serves in the place of the old iron pipe. A cement drinking basin has been provided for wandering horses and burros. Quail and other small birds come here to drink, and to eat the seeds of the desert brush that grows thickly

about the spring; and stubby antelope ground squirrels scurry near-by.
❖ Where the road turns at 5.8 m. is Rock Cave (R), a shallow cavern in a huge rock blackened with smoke. Successive generations of prospectors walled up the cave; under a crevice in the rock that served as a chimney, they built a fireplace over which their beans and sourdough cakes were cooked. The Park Service has cleared away the signs of human occupancy.

Middle Spring, in the gully (R), has a small flow of good water.
❖ The Cyanide Mill, 6.4 m. above the road, mills ore from several mines. Gray residue from the mill has coated the slope below.
❖ The road winds up the canyon to emerge on Harrisburg Flats (alt. 4500), 9.5 m.; the peak directly ahead is Telescope.
❖ At 10.3 m. is a junction with a dirt road.

Left on this road to the Site of Skidoo (alt. 5500), 8 m. Only two small houses remain of a town that had a population of 500 in 1907, a school for its 20 children, a newspaper, and a telephone line crossing Death Valley to Rhyolite. The Skidoo claim was found during the Rhyolite boom by three tenderfeet, who sold out to Bob Montgomery of Rhyolite for $60,000. it was considered a success because, for each dollar spent in development, two were taken out. The gross was probably somewhere between three and six million dollars. The town of Skidoo was as wild and lawless as most mining towns. When Johnny Ramsey, friend of all the town and a storekeeper who had grubstaked dozens of prospectors, was stabbed and killed, the citizens acted quickly. The county seat was at Lone Pine, 50 miles away over rough roads, and the citizens of Skidoo were suspicious of the Lone Pine brand of justice; so they hanged the killer themselves to make sure it would be done. The day after the body had been cut down, they strung it up again for the convenience of a photographer. This was probably the only hanging in the area, for Skidoo became known as the town that had had a hanging.

The red, old-fashioned, verandaed Administration Building, 8.5 m., is perched high above the Valley. Southwest over the hill is the Million-Dollar Slope, from which a million dollars was taken. Judge William B. Gray of Beatty, who now owns the property, once said that the gold ore, some running as high as $30,000 a ton, could be scooped out into wheelbarrows. The present work-ings are northeast of the Administration Building. The old Stamp Mill in the canyon below the building was run by water piped 20 miles in from Telescope. When prices were high as a result of the World War the pipe line was sold, and today all water must be trucked in.

Below the main highway, old, little-used roads wind about Harrisburg Flats. While Skidoo was in full operation, a herd of 1400 goats browsed here, receiving water from the pipe line; they constituted Skidoo's fresh meat supply. Almost all supplies, including fresh vege-tables with lumps of ice tucked in among them to keep them fresh during the Death Valley crossing, were freighted from Rhyolite.

❖ At 11.7 m. is a junction with a dirt road.

Left on this road to the Site of Harrisburg, 2 m., a long-vanished tent town named for Shorty Harris, who with Pete Auguerre-berry made the strike here July 4, 1905. There was not much ore and the town quickly died. Harris, a stocky man with a mouthful of gold teeth, is said to have been one of the most genial and entertaining liars of the desert. His grave is in Death Valley (see Tour 4).

Auguerreberry Point (alt. 6000), 6 m., named for Pete Auguerreberry, a miner and prospector who laid out the first road, is an unusually advantageous place from which to see Death Valley in the afternoon. A short path leads from the parking place to View Point. Far below, in the white floor, is the dark rectangle of Furnace Creek Ranch; directly opposite the lookout, the brindled Funeral Mountains rear up to eye level. From Boundary Canyon (L), between the Funerals and the Grapevines, an alluvial fan sweeps toward the Salt Marshes. Beyond the white Clay Beds (L), the Grapevines curve toward the northern end of the Valley; Charleston Peak (alt. 11,910) is 80 miles to the east in Nevada. On a brilliant day the desert ranges are pink and tawny, lavender and brown.

❖ South of Harrisburg Flats the road rises to Emigrant Pass (alt. 5320), curves around the hills, and descends through a narrow, winding defile into Wildrose Canyon, 20.4 m.

Augereberry Point (6240 feet) offers visitors a sweeping view of Death Valley National Monument. A short trail leads to a view of the salt pan and the steep, rugged country that makes up the Panamint Mountain Range.

Left here on an oiled road to the Park Service Summer Head-quarters 0.3 m., occupied from May 1 to September 1, when Death Valley scorches in the sun. East of the headquarters the road, now dirt, rises on a stiff grade through upper Wildrose Canyon (impassable when there is snow on the road).

There are many ore deposits in Wildrose Canyon. For a number of years the ore was smelted in small, square stone furnaces. A few mines are still worked; threadlike roads run up the hills (L) to the buildings, and finer threads run from the buildings to the workings.

On the hills (R) at 3.4 m. is a scar, faint but still discernible, left by the pipe line that carried water from Telescope to Skidoo. The scar is more clearly marked on the opposite hills.

Along the western horizon stretches the full length of the High Sierra, a curved mass of fawn granite, flecked with snow patches. Below the Sierra are (R) the Inyo Mountains. Beyond the dun shoulders of the Panamints in the foreground is the blue and purple Argus Range, the west wall of Panamint Valley.

From below, the high Panamints appear to be covered with

Charcoal Kilns, Upper Wildrose Canyon

brush. They are, as a matter of fact, well wooded above 6000 feet. Fragrant junipers come first, then pines, then, higher, mountain mahogany, with gray foliage and curling fragrant tassels; and last are bristlecone and limber pines.

The 10 Charcoal Kilns, 7.3 m., are large stone beehive structures; they have been standing idle since the 1870s, when they were used in making charcoal from the pines that grew thickly here. The charcoal was freighted across Panamint Valley to the Modoc Mine for use in smelting ore. The floors of the kilns are thickly strewn with bits of charcoal, and a smoky odor still clings to the rough walls.

This section of the road is fairly steep (second or low gear necessary; it is well to carry water, for most cars boil furiously).

Thorndike's (alt. 7500), 8 m., is the home of a man who has lived for many years in the region.

Mahogany Flats (alt. 8133), 8.5 m., on a saddle of the Panamints, is the end of the automobile road.

1. Left here on a foot trail 0.1 m. to a Picnic Ground and Viewpoint. Stocky, nut-bearing piñons that seem enormous when seen after leaving the treeless desert below, cover the saddle. Formerly this was a favorite food-gathering place of the Indians. East, just below the ridge is the deep, curved trough of Death Valley, and west is Panamint Valley, a small edition of Death Valley but approximately 2000 feet higher.

2. Right from Mahogany Flats on a well-graded foot trail that skirts the east side of Manly Peak (alt. 10,000), named for Lewis Manly, scout of the Bennett-Arcane party. The trail crosses the saddle and switchbacks up the west face of Telescope Peak to the summit, 6 m. Telescope, from the edge of its alluvial fan in Death Valley to the tip, measures more than 11,300 feet. The peak, named in 1860 by W.T. Henderson, the first white man to ascend it, was so called because only through a telescope had he ever seen so far. The view from the summit is utterly magnificent. Far below, Death Valley swims in the heat haze and colored desert ranges, row upon row, lie baking in the sun. The blue Sierra (W) is high on the horizon; beyond the Owlshead Mountains (S) is the flat top of Pilot

Knob, for many years a landmark for freighters toiling over the desert. Farther south is the San Gabriel Range near Los Angeles. East are the Charlestons, and north, beyond the Panamints, is the Last Chance Range.

❖ Wildrose Springs (alt. 3617), 21.7 m., was named Rose Spring in 1860 by the George party for the roses blooming here. Some more meticulous person added the prefix. On Christmas Day, near-by, the party found antimony deposits, which they named the Christmas Gift. The springs are in a little hollow in the rocks that has been walled in for protection.

❖ South of Wildrose Station (gas, meals, grocery store), 22.3 m., the road follows a narrow canyon, carved by water spilled from the wide basin of upper Wildrose Canyon. As the road leaves the winding walls, Panamint Valley and the southern end of the Argus Range are visible. In prehistoric times Panamint Valley was a lake fed from Searles Lake, which in turn was fed from Owens Valley. Salt deposits in the center of the Valley indicate where the last evaporation of the water took place. From the 1860s on, mines have been worked in the surrounding ranges. The roads leading to these mines are mostly steep and rough.

❖ The main road continues through low alluvial hills; the oiled surface ends at the boundary of the Monument, 25.1 m.

❖ At 30.9 m. is a junction with a rough dirt road.

Right on this rough road, crossing the Slate Range, to Trona, 60 m.

The main road swings near this junction toward the mountains. The massive, dappled Panamints rise more than 8000 feet above the flat rubble floor to Manly, Rogers, and Telescope Peaks. South of Telescope the ridge slopes toward the Slate Range.

❖ The Indian Ranch, 38.5 m., is the home of Panamint George, a handsome, white-haired old Indian, who knew most of the white men who came here in the early days. He guided Doctor George in 1860, and assumed his name. The ranch is surrounded by a fence made of barbwire, old iron wagon tires, and other odds and ends. Mesquite, willow, tamarisk, and grass flourish in the subsurface water that flows from Hall Canyon (L). Where the road turns the corner of the ranch are two small houses and some cottonwood and poplar trees. The old

Stage Coach in the yard miraculously survived the days when, drawn by four sturdy horses, it tore across long stretches of desert, wound through canyons, and bumped over rough mountains, carrying mustachioed and booted gentlemen from Randsburg and Lone Pine to Skidoo and Ballarat.

South of the ranch the road crosses a foot-wide stream—a stream that would be hardly noticeable elsewhere, but is of vast importance in this arid country—and follows the base of the mountains around a marshy flat, where willows and mesquite grow thickly.

❖ At 39.9 m. the full length of the Argus Range, western wall of Panamint Valley, is in view. Maturango Peak (alt. 8850), directly opposite, is the highest point in the range, which runs due north and south from Darwin Wash to Searles Lake. The two most famous mines in this range are the old Modoc, which belonged to George Hearst, father of William Randolph Hearst, and the Minietta, which is still being worked. Down the Valley (L) is what seems to be a small cliff, running from a canyon out into the valley. This is the Ballarat Fan, a recent fault, geologically speaking. The sides of the Panamints, deeply eroded, look as if they had been scored with a gigantic wire brush.

❖ At 42.5 m. is a junction with a dirt road.

> Left on this road, which slants up across a broad detrital fan to Surprise Canyon, 3 m., about 3000 feet above sea level at its entrance. The canyon was named in 1860 by S.G. George, who was hunting for the lost Gunsight Mine. George climbed a mile or so up the canyon to the Narrows then, suspicious of his Indian guide, turned back; this guide was Indian George, now owner of the Indian Ranch. The road clings to the canyon side, and though narrow is in fair condition.
>
> Chris Wicht's Camp (cabins $1) (R), 4.5 m., lies in a hollow of the hills. Cottonwood trees rustle here and chickens scratch in the moist earth around them. A stream, circling the triangular bit of ground, supplies power for 9 electric lights, and runs into a swimming pool, 75 feet long. Chris says he built the pool "big enough so a frog could get a swim." The sturdy ex-mayor of Ballarat, singlehanded, has built his house, cabins, and swimming pool, and finds time to repair the road each spring, after the water from 30 square miles of mountain basins has roared down

the narrow gorge and taken a few savage bites out of it. (for the rest of this route see Tour 19.)

❖ Ballarat (alt. 1067; est. pop. 10), 44.1 m., only a few houses (no facilities; water) squatting below the beautiful fawn Panamints, is all that remains of a former hustling, bustling town with 400 or 500 inhabitants. Ballarat was not a mining town in itself, though there were mines in the canyons just east of it; it was rather a supply center for the entire district, and a place for hilarious relief from hard work in the mines.

It was at one of the mines near-by that a harassed owner came around the end of the cook house to find a burro with its head poked through the kitchen window. "And do you know," he said, "the cook was tough and hardboiled that I—me, the owner—couldn't go into that cook house half an hour late and get breakfast—the cook wouldn't stand for it. And yet there he stood, 6 feet tall and weighing 200 pounds and all of it bone and muscle, making little hot cakes, one by one, and feeding them to that burro. He looked kind of foolish and said, "I might as well feed this flapjack batter to Hattie as throw it out." That was all right with me, but I said, "Well, why don't you just make one big cake and give it to her all at once?" And do you know, he just said, kind of softlike, "Hattie likes them small."

Chris Wicht's Former Saloon, a mecca for miners, on the corner (L), is a long wooden building with adobe front and tin roof. Several adobe houses near-by are melting into the ground; some have boarded up windows and doors, but a few houses, in good condition, are still occupied. Shorty Harris, the prospector, made his headquarters in one of these small adobe houses until his death a few years ago. Spread out on the desert are the remnants of other houses, broken bottles, and junk.

The stage from Johannesburg climbed over the Slate Mountains on a road that no automobile could ever negotiate; most of Skidoo's supplies were hauled over that road by mules.

At Ballarat is the junction with a rough road (see Tour 20) leading to Goler Wash, Wingate Pass, and Lone Willow Spring.

❖ Here also is the junction with a road that climbs the Slate Range to reach Trona, 23 m.

Rough Road Tours

Special Information

Update:
❖ The following tips still apply.
❖ Remember to always start out any desert journey with plenty of gas, water, food and good, up-to-date maps.
❖ Always check with park rangers regarding road and weather conditions before embarking on a trip.
❖ Do not drive off designated roads.

❖ Latest information on road conditions should be obtained from Park Service officials since these roads are sometimes impassable.
❖ Automobiles should be in sound condition, with good tires and at least one spare. These roads are hard on rubber.
❖ An adequate supply of water should be carried, for the traveler and for the radiator; also gas, oil, and food. There are no gas stations or lunch stands along these roads.
❖ Notify the desk clerk in camps and hotels, or a ranger, or National Park Headquarters, before starting on these trips, so that in case of trouble you can be sure of receiving help. It is imperative that you give notice of your return.
❖ It is well for cars to travel in pairs on some trips so that in case of a breakdown there will be transportation for the party.
❖ Little pitches (the desert dweller's name for a short, surging bit of

road that may have a grade of 29 per cent), gullies, and sharp ascents from washes must be taken slowly; otherwise the transmission may be damaged by striking the road or a rock.

❖ Remember that on upgrades the climbing car always has the right-of-way. If you are descending and are near a turnout when you see or hear another car coming on a narrow road, draw to one side and wait till the car passes. Do not count on finding another passing place.

❖ Never hurry! Do not force a car in high; it heats the engine. Grades are often more easily driven in second.

❖ During the warm weather, steep grades should be ascended in the morning. A following wind blows up canyons and slopes during the afternoon, making it difficult to keep engines cool in the still air that surrounds a car traveling in such a wind.

❖ In sand, stay in the ruts and drive steadily; do not apply power suddenly, thus digging the rear wheels in. If wheels sink into the sand and the car will not move, clear away the sand and throw a canvas tarpaulin or brush in front of the wheels to obtain traction.

❖ Be careful in crossing dry lakes. The surface clay sometimes looks dry when it is very soft just below the crust.

❖ The rough roads of Death Valley lead into isolated back country; scattered through it are old mines, ghost towns, and rocks with prehistoric inscriptions. Some roads end at cabins where prospectors and miners live. They are pleasant men with an understanding of the obsession—which they share—that finds satisfaction in traveling rough roads across desert land. Some of the roads are usually little more than wheel tracks or faint ruts. They swing off the main highways to wind through washes and valleys and to scramble up and down steep canyons.

Tour 8:

Junction with Calif. 190—Echo Canyon—Schwaub
9 m.

Update:

❖ Route is recommended for 4WD only.
❖ There is no longer a gate marking the road.
❖ Window Rock is called "Needle's Eye" today.
❖ At the 8 mile point are the remains of the Inyo Gold Mining Company, and an interpretive sign.
❖ The remains of Schwaub are actually located in the next canyon over. ·
❖ Camping is not allowed on the first four miles of the road.

Sandy, soft gravel; steep grades.

❖ The Echo Canyon Road branches north from Calif. 190, 0 m., in Furnace Creek Wash, 2 miles east of Furnace Creek Junction (see Tour 1, sec. b), goes through a gate, and crosses the wash before beginning to climb up shadowy Echo Canyon. The road is steep and winding, and the soft gravel gives poor traction; but in early fall and late spring, when central Death Valley is oppressive during the middle of the day, this route provides a delightful trip into cooler air. At about 5 m. Window Rock, with a hole cut by erosion, can be seen.
❖ At about 7 m. is a junction with a road.

Left on this road to a Viewpoint, 1.5 m., from which the northern end of Death Valley is visible.

Schwaub, 9 m., is an old mining camp with a few deserted and tumbling houses and one or two that are still inhabited.

Tour 9:

Stove Pipe Wells Hotel—Mesquite Flat

8.5 m.

Update:

❖ This rough-road tour is recommended for 4WD only.
❖ Any cultural artifacts must be left undisturbed.

Sandy road, easy grades in valley; steep rocky road to Cottonwood Canyon.

❖ This sandy, rough road runs north from Stove Pipe Wells Hotel, 0 m. (see Tour 1, sec. b), on Calif. 190, and skirts the west side of Death Valley. The sand on this road is frequently deep and soft; slow, careful driving is necessary.

❖ At 2.5 m. is a junction with a rocky road.

Left approximately 4 m. on this road up the detrital fan toward the Panamints. The car should be parked as soon as the road becomes very rough; the rest of the trip must be made on foot. A narrow entrance leads into a wide basin.

1. Left is Cottonwood Canyon, a deep gash running almost due south into the Panamints (4 to 8 hours required for exploration). Well up the canyon is a small stream that waters many large cottonwood trees; quail and sheep often come here. Fifteen or 20 years ago a number of trees were washed out by a heavy cloudburst and carried to the center of Death Valley, where for some years their bleached trunks lay.

2. Right from Cottonwood Canyon through a smaller opening

Annie Shoshone grinding mesquite beans

in the wide basin to Marble Canyon. The surface is very rough, but there are pictographs at the head of the canyon.

❖ North of the road to Cottonwood Canyon is Mesquite Flat. 8.5 m., named for the large mesquite bushes that flourish in the sand dunes. An old Indian trail from Owens Valley came through Saline Valley to Cottonwood Canyon, crossed Death Valley, and continued through Titus Canyon or Daylight Pass to Nevada. Sitting under rude shelters in the mesquite here, the Indians shaped obsidian (volcanic glass) and flint into arrowheads and skinning knives. The small-game arrowheads were usually retrieved, but large war arrowheads are often found on old Indian battlefields. A few delicate game arrowheads have been sifted from the sand here, and under the bushes are many pieces of black and purple obsidian, and bits of red and white flint.

Just south of the dunes is a large area in which a formal pattern has been outlined with flat pebbles; the whole is a great circle of small rocks. This is supposed to have been made by Indians.

Tour 10:

Darwin—Junction with Calif. 190

12.8 m. Zinc Hill Road

Update:

- ❖ There is still some mining activity in the Darwin area; heed all signs and be sensitive to private property rights.
- ❖ Darwin Falls still remains a refreshing sight in this arid land.
- ❖ Panamint Springs Motel is now known as the Panamint Springs Resort.

Narrow dirt road; grades.

❖ The Zinc Hill Road goes northeast out of Darwin, 0 m. (see Tour 1, sec. c), and climbs a short, steep road up Lane Hill. At the top of the hill, a sharp turn (R) discloses a magnificent and far-reaching view. The crumpled mountains—tan, brown, and green—flow down to a patch of white, which is Panamint Valley, 12 miles away and 3000 feet below. West, beyond the valley, are the reds and purples of the Panamint Range. The short stretch of road beyond the summit of Lane Hill has a 27 per cent grade, and should be taken in low gear.

❖ Big buckets swing by on the overhead tram wire of the Darwin Lead Mine, 1.5 m., carrying ore from the mine to the reduction plant, just west of Darwin (see Tour 1, sec. c). The mine workings and cabins are around the shoulder of the mountain at 2 m.

❖ The Darwin Lead Mine Pumping Plant (L), 6 m., supplies the Darwin works with water. Just beyond the plant the road winds and ascends sharply out of the wash, offering views of the wash below and of mountains beyond them, striated with ocher of many shades.

❖ Below the crest (alt. 4500), 7.5 m., is Panamint Valley, with the Panamint Range on its western side rising at one point to 11,045 feet. The road now descends the flanks of Zinc Hill, curving sharply backward and forward.

❖ Halfway down the hill are deserted buildings around an old Zinc Mine, 8.5m. Just beyond the mine is a sign warning drivers to go into low gear on the Zinc Hill Grade, which is steep, narrow, and has many sharp turns; the turns have been widened into the bank to afford passing places (a climbing car has the right-of-way).

❖ At 10.5 m. is a junction with a dirt road.

> Left on this road to Darwin Falls, 0.5 m. These falls are never dry, and the water supply for Darwin is hauled from this point. Long ago, when Darwin was a booming town, a Chinese had a vegetable garden in a rich patch of earth just below the falls. He did a flourishing business in Darwin until a cloudburst washed away his vegetables and trees, and the rich earth, too. Stone basins in the wash, worn by flood water, are frequently filled with very clear, icy water; hardy souls bathe in them.

Below the Darwin Falls road, the tiny stream from the falls disappears into the sand.

The desert wind whispers in the canyon, and sways the flowers lightly; in spring evening primroses fill the air with their fragrance. Occasionally a chuckwalla is seen sunning himself on a warm rock. In 1927, when there was a road camp in Darwin Wash, fresh meat was scarce, and the men grumbled about the eternal beans and salt pork. Suddenly the cook began giving them appetizing stews containing pieces of meat. The camp was peaceful until the day when one of the men went behind the cook tent and saw the horned heads and the skins of large chuckwallas. The cook left camp suddenly, traveling up the canyon in a cloud of dust.

❖ At 12.8 m. is a junction with Calif. 190 (see Tour 1, sec. c). by Panamint Motel.

Tour 11:
Junction with Greenwater Valley Road—
Greenwater Canyon—Death Valley Junction
18.2 m.

Update:

❖ This tour is for 4WD only.
❖ All cultural artifacts must be left undisturbed; damage to some petroglyphs in the area can be seen here.
❖ The ladders mentioned are long-gone.

Sandy rough road.

❖ The Greenwater Canyon road branches east from Greenwater Valley Road, 0 m. (see Tour 2), 15.6 miles south of the junction with Calif. 190. Where the road curves around a spur of the Black Mountains, 1 m., is the entrance to a canyon.

Left here on a short trail that leads into the canyon to a group of Petroglyphs. These rock pictures—gray outlines—have been made by chipping away the dark brown desert varnish on the rocks. The brown surface is very hard and is chipped with great difficulty.

❖ The main road winds gently down the canyon between rough, dark mountains. More Petroglyphs are in a small open space (L), 3.6 m., beside the road. A number of designs, most of them symmetrical, have been chipped on boulders; many are composed of concentric circles; a few look very much like desert tortoises.

❖ At 5.2 m. is a junction with a foot trail.

> Left on this trail 0.5 m. up a rocky canyon to a large basin (R), gouged out of the mountain by storms. Here a stone waterfall, now dry, can be climbed by two ladders. At the head of the fall, trails lead to four shallow caves where are Pictographs and Petroglyphs in good condition. The paintings are in red and black. Scattered among designs that the modern Shoshone do not understand are men on horseback, spirited dancing men, deer and sheep. Though the present-day Indians do not know who made these drawings, those of men on horseback must have been made after the coming of the Spaniards in 1769; there were no horses in California before that, except in the prehistoric past.

East of the junction with the trail leading to the petroglyphs the main road winds down the wash between hills of milky clays thinly covered with dark brown rocks, and emerges on the smooth slope of the Amargosa Desert. (There are gullies and chuck holes filled with dust here; drive with care.) The Lila C Mine (R) was the first colemanite mine in the region; here also was the first site of the town of Ryan (See Tour 2). The oddly striped peak to the southeast is Eagle Mountain.

❖ At 17.2 m. is the junction with Calif. 127; left here to Death Valley Junction, 18.2 m. (see Tour 1, sec. a).

Tour 12:

Junction with East Highway—Cave Springs

55 m. Cave Springs Road

Update:

❖ Alas, this tour is now a part of the China Lake Naval Weapons Center and cannot be taken.

Roadbed partly improved; some steep grades.

❖ The Cave Springs Road, branching southwest from East Highway, 0 m. (See Tour 3), in southern Death Valley, at a point 10 miles northwest of Saratoga Springs Junction, is the shortest route between Barstow and Death Valley; along the route are still a few old road signs erected many years ago by the Geological Survey. Some of these are so rusty that it is difficult to read names and mileages, but what can be discerned is accurate.

❖ The Cave Springs Road ascends the big wash of the Avawatz Mountains, passes Denning Spring, and then climbs to Cave Spring (approx. alt. 3900), 10 m. Here, deep in the solid rock, are caves blasted by Adrian Egbert. In them are little streams and cool pools, fed by a spring inside the mountain. Even when the temperature is 120° F. outside, the air behind the curtain that hangs over the cave mouth is cool; the inner caves are almost chilly.

❖ The road drops from Avawatz Pass (alt. 4315), 12.5 m., then climbs again to Granite Pass (alt. 4255) in the Granite Mountains. Below Granite Pass the reddish mountains of the Mojave Desert rise from a tawny flat surface. The road crosses Bicycle Lake (dry) at the foot of the Tierfort Mountains; then Coyote Lake (dry), near the Calico Mountains, to a junction with U.S. 91-466, 42 m.; R. on U.S. 91-466. Yermo is at 43 m. and Barstow at 55 m. (approx.).

Tour 13:

Junction with West Highway—Hanaupah Canyon
6 m.

Update:

❖ Recommended for 4WD only.
❖ Several springs are located in the canyon.
❖ At the end of the road is an old road leading to the Peon Mine.

Steep grade. This tour should be taken in the morning to avoid the following wind, which usually blows up the canyons in the afternoon.

❖ The Hanaupah Canyon road branches west from the West Highway, 0 m. (see Tour 4), 1.7 miles north of Shorty Harris's Grave, and climbs the detrital fan nearly to the mouth of the canyon. Here it drops down into the wash and then climbs the loose rock and sand bed of Hanaupah Canyon until it reaches an altitude of 4500 feet. In the upper canyon a stream of water tumbles down, but is lost in the sandy surface. Lusty grapevines, willows, and clematis grow in a tangle, and a profusion of wild flowers blooms here in April and May.

Tour 14:

Junction with West Highway—Warm Spring
Canyon—Butte Valley—Anvil Spring—Goler
Wash—Panamint Valley

30 m.

Update:

❖ West Highway is now called West Side Road.
❖ Tour for 4WD only; the road is very rough. Use great care;
watch for washouts and other vehicles, especially on the
narrow stretches.
❖ The tents at Warm Springs have been replaced with buildings
that are now closed.
❖ Do not disturb the mining equipment along the road or the
talc mine remains.
❖ Several cabins are located in Butte Valley, including one called
"the geologist's cabin," because it's made of stones.
❖ Carl Mengel's gravesite is marked with a plaque at the top of
Mengel Pass.
❖ The Wingate Pass option can no longer be taken, since it is
now part of the China Lake Naval Weapons Center.

Rough road with high centers; steep grades. Route for experienced
desert drivers only; it is advisable to have more than one car in party
following the route.

❖ The Warm Spring Canyon Road turns west from the West Highway, 0 m. (see Tour 4), 13 miles south of Bennett's Well, and ascends

the low foothills of the Panamints; as it rises above Death Valley it presents far-sweeping views to the north and to the south. The road rambles over the hills (alt. 1500) for about 3 miles, then drops into the wash of Warm Spring Canyon. The low, bordering brown hills of the canyon are striped here and there with layers of white talc. Many holes have been dug in the sides of the canyon by men hunting for a deposit of pure talc.

❖ Warm Spring (alt. 3000), 11.3 m., is in a gully just above a group of tents and huge fig trees. The tents and machinery belong to a company leasing the spring from its Indian owner and working a mine in a small canyon (R). A reservoir below the spring holds the water used in the mining operations and also serves as a swimming pool. Quail feed around the spring in spite of the fact that red-tailed hawks lie in wait here and pounce as the quail move from bush to bush. The fig trees, planted 40 years ago, have made the stone terrace under them a cool, green haven in hot weather. A tiny patch of lawn before the cook tent is guarded by a blue and white enamel sign that warns "Keep off the grass." At dusk burros are often seen racing at full tilt down the hill to the cook tent for kitchen scraps.

❖ West of Warm Spring the road is rough, with large rocks here and there (drive with care). At 16 m. the road turns, still ascending, into Butte Valley (alt. 4500), which is ringed by the Panamints. Small birds and rodents go busily about their affairs here, with eyes alert for the golden eagles and the red-tailed hawks that often float high above in the clear air. The brushy valley is crisscrossed with tiny trails worn by small rodent feet.

In Butte Valley any of several wheel tracks can be followed, but the Warm Spring Road and the Goler Wash Road (See Tour 20), from lower Panamint Valley are the only ones that are safe for entrance into and exit from Butte Valley.

The weary forty-niners may have been the first white people to see the solid mass of rock, stratified in dark grays and tans and yellows, that protrudes from the smooth, sloping valley floor. In the 1860s Hugh McCormack crossed the Panamints here and named the mass Curious Butte; this was later changed to Striped Butte. To the south, high on the mountainside and small when seen from a distance through the clear air, are buildings around a mill that produces a high-grade concentrate of gold, lead, and silver. The concentrate is shipped out to a smelter.

❖ Several roads lead to Anvil Spring, approx. 24 m., which is on the south side of Butte Valley. A big cottonwood tree here shades a little shack owned by a geologist; behind and above the tree is the spring, forming a tiny pond in a clump of bright green brush. It is fenced to keep burros from trampling in it, but even at that its water is probably not safe for human consumption.

❖ Greater View Spring, 24.5 m., is the home of Carl Mengel, once a prospecting partner of Shorty Harris. The view for which the spring is named is eastward, over the Funeral Mountains; it is one of the wide, far-reaching panoramas typical of the Death Valley region. The big cottonwood trees here, 45 years old, are near Mengel's neat white-washed stone house, which has 18-inch walls that are rather successful non-conductors of heat and cold. In 1912 Carl Mengel bought the Oro Fino claim in Goler Wash. At that time ore from the mine had to be carried out on mules; while Mengel was trying to find a better trail down to Panamint Valley, he picked up a piece of float in Goler Wash. He panned it by the light of a campfire and found the ore so rich in gold that he stopped looking for an easier trail from his old claim, and went to work on the new one the very next morning. The ore was rich—some of it ran $35,000 a ton—but the deposit was small.

❖ South of Greater Valley Spring is a rough, steep road that goes down Goler Wash to lower Panamint Valley, 30 m. A loop trip to Death Valley can be made by two routes, one through lower Panamint Valley (see Tours 20 and 7) and the other through Wingate Pass (see Tour 15).

Tour 15:

Junction with West Highway—Wingate Pass—
Panamint Valley

9 m.

Update:

❖ This tour can no longer be taken. The Wingate Pass Road is now contained within the China Lake Naval Weapons Center.

Rough hard road; high center. Only for experienced desert drivers; when possible two or more cars should travel together.

❖ The Wingate Pass road branches southwest from the West Highway, 0 m. (see Tour 4), in southern Death Valley at a point 4.6 miles northwest of Ashford Junction. It ascends the rugged slopes of Wingate Wash. The total rise from Death Valley is only a little more than 2000 feet, and there are no steep grades. Broad Wingate Pass, reached at 12 m., seems peaceful and friendly when contrasted with the savage magnificence of Death Valley. About 5 miles wide and 10 miles long, the pass connects Death Valley and Panamint Valley. It was named Windy Gap in the 1880s, when it was part of the borax route, because there was always a wind here to flatten the mules' long ears and fling dust and gravel into the faces of the drivers and swampers. Wingate Pass is one of the natural entrances to Death Valley, but the rain that falls in the mountains tears up roads on the slopes. With the passing of wagon freighting, no economic reason remained for the development of a main route through the pass.

❖ The Monorail (see below), approx. 14 m., strides over Wingate Pass with long wooden legs on its way to the summit of Layton Pass. Although it was built in 1923, its unpainted wood is still fresh in appearance.

❖ At 14 m. is a junction with a dirt road.

Left on this road to the Epsom Salts Works (alt. 2500), 3 m., in a little bay of the hills. There is a white surface deposit of Epsom salts here, and the promoters believed that large profits would be forthcoming if the salts could be conveyed cheaply to the railroad, 30 or miles west. Some enthusiastic person designed the monorail, which was to provide cheap transportation. The rail, mounted on caliper legs, carried two cars, one on each side, which a tractor dragged up- and down-hill to the railroad at Trona. But a multitude of unforeseen difficulties made the monorail something of a nightmare, and when the Epsom salts were found to contain too much desert dust, the works were closed. Several further attempts have been made to capitalize on the large deposit of salts, but none has succeeded.

On the same road, south of the Epsom Salts Works, is a junction with a dirt road, 12 m.; left on this road 0.2 m. to Hidden Spring. The board covering the spring is now loose and warped; leaves fill the basin, and now and then the body of some small animal is fished out of it. When borax was being hauled from the Harmony Borax Works to Mojave, the tank wagon for the rest camp in Wingate Pass would be brought here to be filled. Quail and doves call and coo on the slopes here, and small birds chirp from the bushes.

❖ West of the Epsom Salts road in Wingate Pass, the road continues southwest across the mesa and descends the blunt eastern end of the pass into Panamint Valley, 25 m. (see Tour 20). The return trip to Death Valley can be made by way of Wildrose Canyon (see Tour 7).

Tour 16:

Junction with Beatty Road—Leadfield—Titus
Canyon—Junction with Ubehebe Crater Road
26 m.

Update:

❖ This road is closed with a locked gate during the summer
months.
❖ Check with park rangers regarding weather and road conditions before taking this road.
❖ Recommended for 4WD.

One-way road, grades; soft gravel in Titus Canyon.

Before attempting to follow this road inquire at Park Service Headquarters about road conditions; storms often make road impassable.

❖ The Leadfield Road branches north from the Beatty Road, 0 m. (see
Tour 5), at a point on the Amargosa Desert 3.8 miles southwest of
Rhyolite. It runs toward the Grapevine peaks, crosses a divide, drops
down into a deep bowl, and climbs again to brilliant Red Pass (alt.
5500), 12 m.

❖ The road winds down into the ghost town of Leadfield (alt. 4500),
15 m., which boomed in 1925 and 1926, as a result of the skillful work
of a promoter who controlled a large deposit of very low-grade lead
ore. Groups of investors were brought in for inspection tours, and
soon a town was built in the deep canyon, which is so narrow that
there was just room enough for two lines along a single street. When
no more people could be lured to investment, by the aid of full-page

Titus Canyon

advertisements and other devices, Leadfield swiftly passed from 24-hour activity to desert silence. Within a few years thrifty desert men had carted away most of the houses for use in more accessible places. Only a few walls and foundations are now left to mark the site of the briefly noisy town.

❖ North of Leadfield the road enters the upper mouth of Titus Canyon, 24 m., which was named for Morris Titus, a young engineer who left Rhyolite with a prospecting party in the boom days. While they were encamped here, their water gave out; Titus left in search of water and help, but was never seen again.

Titus Canyon is a narrow, deep slit in the mountains—its walls are only 15 to 40 feet apart, and rise sheerly for 500 feet. The upper walls are rugged, but the lower 40 feet apart, and rise sheerly for 500 feet. The upper walls are rugged, but the lower 40 feet exhibit smooth bands that were made by water-borne gravel. The Titus Canyon Road, a road by courtesy only, winds down the soft gravel bed between boulders that make careful driving imperative. When the Leadfield ore was first discovered this was the only way into and out of the area.

Titus Canyon, circa 1930s

Supplies for the mines and the town had to be brought in through Death Valley and patiently hauled up this difficult route, with a rise of 5500 feet in 11 miles.

❖ Klare Spring, 17.5 m., is marked by a patch of tules. When Leadfield was alive, some enterprising soul mounted a 50-gallon drum on a platform here and marked it with a sign saying "Shower baths, 25¢." Dusty men stood below a pipe in the bottom of the platform, while the owner released a limited amount of water over them. He made money, for there was very little water in Leadfield.

In the lower part of Titus Canyon the dark walls are streaked with white marble and decorated with a few Indian Pictographs. The road rounds a final sharp turn, and Tin Mountain in Death Valley comes into view, framed by the walls of the narrow canyon. From the canyon mouth the road descends the alluvial slope to join the Ubehebe Crater Road, 26 m. (see Tour 6), in upper Death Valley 15.4 miles north of its junction with Calif. 190.

Tour 17:
Junction with Beatty Road—Chloride City/Cliffs
21.5 m.

Update:

❖ Recommended for 4WD only.
❖ The Chloride City road is marked by a cattleguard.
❖ The remarkable view at the end is well-worth the trip.

Steep grades.

❖ The Chloride City road branches southeast from the Beatty Road, 0 m. (see Tour 5), on the Amargosa Desert, at a point 3.8 miles southwest of Rhyolite, crosses the Amargosa Desert, climbs a shallow canyon, heads toward the top of the Funeral Range, makes a sharp turn (L) for a brief steep climb high above Death Valley, and turns into a shallow basin surrounded by peaks of the Funerals (L).

❖ Chloride City (alt. 5000), 20 m., in the shallow basin, is shrinking away under weather and years. Only a few buildings are left. At one time there were a superintendent's house, a blacksmith shop, an assay house, and bunkhouse and cook houses. Water for the inhabitants and for mining operations was pumped from Keane Springs (see Tour 5), and it was so precious that a watchman was hired to walk up and down the pipe line and guard against leaks.

❖ South of Chloride City the road leads to a saddle, 21.5 m., from which a foot trail goes on to Chloride Cliff. The view from the latter is well worth the effort expended on the trip. Beyond the tawny Panamints, on a clear day, a 100-mile line of the high Sierra Nevada is visible from Mount Whitney to the Minarets near Yosemite Valley; perhaps more of Death Valley can be seen from this point than from any other viewpoint on the rim.

144

Tour 18:

Junction with Ubehebe Crater Road—Sand Spring
15 m.

Update:

❖ The road has improved greatly since this was written. Today it is a mixture of good dirt and some paved sections. Known as Death Valley Road or Big Pine Road, when taken to the northwest, it leads all the way to Big Pine.

Rough, sandy road; no steep grades.

For experienced desert drivers only; preferably with two cars. Only about 12 cars a year use route. Advisable only for Death Valley.
❖ The road to Sand Spring branches north from the entrance of the one-way road section of Ubehebe Crater Road, 0 m. (see Tour 6); it is a sandy, twisting route that climbs steadily, but there are no steep grades. Around Sand Spring (alt. 3128), approx. 15 m., there are the tangles of mesquite usually found wherever there is water, a few lonesome cottonwood trees, and a weather-beaten, windowless and doorless shack that was built by a hopeful homesteader. About the yard lie horned skulls of cattle; Death Valley Scotty nailed one over the door some years ago. Sand Spring is pleasant when the sun shines, for the air is then sweet, and birds chirp and flutter in the mesquite; but on a gray day the sky is too near, the air is heavy, and the sight of the forlorn venture is oppressive.

North of Sand Spring the road, rougher now, runs through Tule Canyon in the Lida Range, passing places where Chinese panned for gold. It continues to Lida, Nevada. (alt. 6033), 23 m.

Tour 19:
Chris Wicht's Camp—Panamint City

4.5 m.

Update:

❖ A 1964 article in "Desert" magazine reported that Chris Wicht's Camp was in poor condition. Since then, the camp has been washed away by successive floods.

❖ Use care in the area; some mining may continue on private property. Obey all signs.

Rough; steep grades.

Road sometimes washed out; inquire at Chris Wicht's Camp.

The Panamint City Road, a continuation of the Surprise Canyon Road, is a side route branching from the Emigrant Canyon-Panamint Valley Road (see Tour 7).

❖ Chris Wicht's Camp (R), 0 m. (see Tour 7), is on a small bench above the road.

❖ The Narrows, 1 m., is a passage, 5 to 15 feet wide, between sloping walls of gray rock. The short stretch of road here usually disappears during the spring rush of water that issues from the large basin above, through this bottle neck. East of the Narrows the canyon widens somewhat; the road climbs steeply up the west slope of the Panamints.

❖ In the shallow, tilted basin of Surprise Valley (alt. 7500), 9 m., fallen stone walls, almost submerged in the brush, mark the place where Panamint City once stood. The tall smokestack of the mill built by Jones and Stewart of Nevada is against the south slope. A little farther up the same slope are 15 or 20 red shacks of a later day. The air is thin and sweet; the quiet is hardly broken by the rustle of small desert life or by the fleeting songs of birds. In 1875 a banner of smoke floated continually from the smokestack, and the air resounded with thump of the stamps in the mill and the clatter of sleds dragging ore down from the mines. Long freight teams snorted and stepped over the wagon chain, in their efforts to turn the great wagons in the single street. Miners came and went on narrow paths carved in the canyon sides. Women with bustles and tilted hats teetered up and down the grade in high-heeled boots. Saloons were roaring pots of laughter, and hurdy-gurdy houses bounced with gaiety. Broad-shouldered William Morris Stewart from Virginia City, with a long, flaming beard, surveyed the hustle and bustle of the town that was to add another million to his wealth.

In 1873 three men had labored up Surprise Canyon, hunting the source of a piece of rich silver float they had picked up in the lower canyon. Where the brushy basin widened they saw gaudy, greenish blue veins of copper-silver ore striping both sides of the cliffs. A fortune hung before their eyes. After they had made several rough assays that showed values as high as $2500 a ton, these three, with several men that had good reason for living in these faraway hills, established the Panamint Mining District. It extended 20 miles along the Panamint Ridge to the center of Death Valley on the east, and on to the center of Panamint Valley on the west.

Word of a new strike drifted out of the high Panamints. The Mother Lode and the Comstock were giving forth millions, and each new strike caused a stampede in the hope that it would reveal more riches. But Panamint, difficult of access, was 60 miles from the nearest road in Owens Valley, and those 60 miles were solid, forbidding ranges. At first only a few men trickled in to investigate the rumors.

In 1874 John P. Jones of Virginia City, who had been active in development in Nevada and had entered the U.S. Senate in 1873, became partner of William Morris Stewart, who had had a part in the development of the Comstock Lode and was completing a term in the Senate. The two men bought a group of claims and formed the Surprise Valley Mill and Water Company. Stewart came here in July to see what they had bought, and activities began at once. In Austin and

Eureka, in Pioche and Pahrump, in San Francisco and on the Mother Lode, in Los Angeles and San Bernardino, men heard that Jones and Stewart owned part of Panamint, and off they started for the new strike, on horseback, on foot, in buggies, and in freight wagons.

Before the end of the year, 700 people puffed and stumbled into the high valley. The town was rough and tough. Many of the citizens were men with notorious pasts. They wore loose guns, and the butcher's two-wheeled cart, the only vehicle that had reached town, carried 57 dead to Sour Dough Gulch, most of these having died of "lead poisoning." Soon a road was cleared somewhat, and express messengers were urging their mounts up it; stages from Lone Pine, Bakersfield, San Bernardino, and Los Angeles were rocking in, clouded with dust; and freight wagons were crawling up, laden with lumber, machinery, and supplies. They rumbled out with ore.

In those days Wells Fargo carried bullion from most of the mines in the West to the mints, issued drafts against the shipment, and carried on a banking business. But after one careful look at the citizens of Panamint City, they flatly refused to carry out bullion; they were too sure that something would happen to it on the long, lonesome route to civilization. Stewart, however, also studied his fellow townsmen, and he shipped out more than a ton of bullion in an open wagon without guards; it had been cast in five huge cannon balls, each one of which weighed 450 pounds.

Panamint City, however, was not destined to be another Virginia City or a Mother Lode. The limestones that enclosed the ore veins was very hard, and expensive to work, and the veins did not long continue their promise of wealth. The bank panic of 1875, squeezing water out of mining stocks, marked the end for Panamint. The stamps thudded on in the mill, but the boom was over. Down the steep road from Panamint went miners, the girls from Maiden Lane, Chinese, saloon and restaurant keepers, the editor and his press, the butcher and his two-wheeled cart. Many went to the new town of Darwin, but some departed east. One eastbound party, that of Isidore Daunet, started across Death Valley in the full heat of summer (see Eagle Borax Works, Tour 4).

Interest in Panamint flickered again in February, 1876, when some small veins of rich ore were discovered, but in July of that same year, a black cloudburst sent tons of water roaring down Main Street. Flimsy shacks were washed away, stone walls were knocked down, and the mill was wrecked. Later the saloons of Ballarat sang of Panamint:

> Her picks are rust,
> Her bones are dust;
> It's forty years
> Since she went bust.

In the years that followed, the jingle of a pack burro's bells was heard now and again coming up the rocky road. Small mines bought beans and bacon for many a man, but there was no other strike. Modern mining methods were tried in 1925, when the two tunnels (R) were driven below the old veins. They were good tunnels, but they did not hit a vein, and in 1926 Panamint was once more a ghost.

In a little canyon above the town (L) is the home of a family that works mines in the district today.

Tour 20:
Ballarat-Lone Willow Spring

37 m.

Update:

❖ Use care to respect signs indicating private property in active mining areas.
❖ Wingate Road south of Goler Wash Road is closed; it is now part of the China Lake Naval Weapons Center.

Road hard and rough.

❖ South of Ballarat (see Tour 7), 0 m., the road runs down the east side of lower Panamint Valley, between the close walls of the Panamint and the Slate Ranges (R). The Slate Range was a mining district in 1861, but the development had only a brief life. Mines in the canyons of the Panamints (L) are reached by roads that ascend the detrital slope in a hit-or-miss way, but in the canyon they scale the walls in bloodcurdling style.
❖ There is an excellent example (L) of an Arrastre (Sp.: *mining mill*) at about 8 m.; it is a round stone basin, 2 feet deep and 6 feet across. Mexican miners used this type of mill, and early American miners also, for it could be constructed almost anywhere of materials on the spot. Cement, wood, and some iron, however, are used in this one. The usual arrastre was a shallow basin of stone or clay to hold ore, which was crushed by two weights. These were suspended from a beam that as a rule was turned round and round by a mule or by a burro—or by the miner himself. A small amount of water converted

the crushed ore to a muddy mixture that flowed out through a trough where quicksilver in catch basins amalgamated with the gold or silver. This crude process, of course, is successful only with free-milling gold or silver.

❖ At 16 m. is a junction with the rough Goler Wash Road (see Tour 14).

❖ At about 25 m. is a junction with the rough, often impassable, Wingate Pass Road (see Tour 15).

The Epsom Salts Monorail (see Tour 15) crosses lower Panamint Valley here, on its way from the summit of the Slate Range.

❖ In the base of the Slate Range is Lone Willow Spring (R) (alt. 3000), approx. 37 m. At this spring was a stage station on the road between San Bernardino and Panamint City; later the place was a rest station on the 20-mule-team route from Death Valley. Some driver, who had been using a willow branch to coax speed from his horses, stuck the branch into moist ground here; the twig flourished and became the willow tree that gave the spring its name. A few piles of rock in the brush mark the sites of cabins.

The road continues south to Granite Wells (water here is foul) and to Randsburg, but it should not be taken by anyone unfamiliar with the country.

APPENDIX

For More Information

Entrance fees (valid for 7-day stay):

$5 per vehicle

$2 per single entry of a person hiking, riding a bus, bike or motorcycle

$15 Annual Park Pass (good for one year at Death Valley)

$25 Golden Eagle Passport (good for one year at any National Park Service area)

Free entrance for Golden Age Passport holders 62 and older, and Golden Access Passport holders (blind or disabled U.S. citizens).

Ranger-led interpretive activities are scheduled regularly at the Visitor Center in Furnace Creek and other locations throughout the park. These activities range from guided hikes through points of historic interest to slide show presentations in the evening—all of which deepen the visitor's understanding of and appreciation for the wonders of Death Valley. Check with the Visitor Center for details and program schedules.

Accommodations in Death Valley

Furnace Creek Ranch (619) 786-2345

Furnace Creek Inn (619) 786-2361 (closed in summer)

Stovepipe Wells Village (619) 786-2387

Services in Death Valley

At Furnace Creek:
Death Valley sightseeing tours (619) 786-2345 Ext. 222
Horseback riding (619) 786-2345
Golf (pro shop) (619) 786-2301
Swimming pool
Service station with four-wheel drive vehicle rental, auto repair and
    towing, camping and trailer services, ice
Restaurants, saloon and snack bars
General store with groceries, ice, gifts, books and apparel
Borax Museum
Death Valley Museum
Laundromat
Post office
Beauty shop
Showers
Sunday interdenominational services

At Stovepipe Wells:
Restaurant and saloon
Service station
General store with groceries, ice, miscellaneous supplies
Gifts, books and apparel
Showers

At Scotty's Castle:
Snack bar
Service station
Gifts, books and apparel

In case of emergency:
Contact Park Ranger, call 911 or (619) 786-2330

CAMPGROUND	Elev.	# of Sites	Fee	Location	Season	Facilities/Notes
Furnace Creek	196'	168	$8.00	Adjacent to Visitor Center	All year	Trailer, motorhome and tent-only sites; water, tables, fireplaces, flush and pit toilets, dump station. Pay showers, laundry, swimming nearby. Note: 14 day limit. For reservations, call (800) 452-1111
Texas Spring	Sea level	93	$5.50	1.5 m. south of Visitor Center	Nov.-April	Trailer, motorhome (generators prohibited), tent-only and group sites; water, tables, fireplaces, flush and pit toilets, dump station. Pay showers, laundry, and swimming pool nearby.
Sunset	190'	1,000	$4.00	1 m. south of Visitor Center	Nov.-April	Primarily for RVs, some tent-only sites; water. No fires. Flush and pit toilets, dump station. Pay showers, laundry, and swimming pool nearby.
Stovepipe Wells	Sea level	200 +	$4.00	Stovepipe Wells Village	Nov.-April	Trailer, motorhome, and tent-only sites; water. No fires. Flush toilets, dump station. Pay showers nearby.
Emigrant	2,100'	10	No fee	9 m. west of Stovepipe Wells Village	April-Oct.	Water, flush toilets. No fires.

CAMPGROUND	Elev.	# of Sites	Fee	Location	Season	Facilities/Notes
Mesquite Springs	1,800'	50	$5.00	4 m. south of Scotty's Castle	All year	Sites for RVs and tents, group sites; water; tables, fireplaces, flush toilets, dump station.
Wildrose	4,100'	30	No fee	56 m. west of Visitor Center	All year	Sites for RVs and tents; tables, fireplaces, pit toilets. No water in winter.
Thorndike	7,500'	8	No fee	8 m. east of Wildrose Campground	Mar.-Nov.	Tables, fireplaces, and pit toilets. Note: Road not passable for trailers, campers, or motorhomes; high-clearance or 4WD may be necessary.
Mahogany Flat	8,200'	10	No fee	9 m. east of Wildrose Campground	Mar.-Nov.	Tables, fireplaces, and pit toilets. Note: Road not passable for trailers, campers, or mothomes; high-clearance or 4WD may be necessary.

Bibliography

Austin, Mary. *Land of Little Rain.* New York, Houghton Mifflin, 1903.
A picture of the beauty, loneliness, and charm of the desert.

Bigler, Henry W. "Extracts from the Journal of Henry W. Bigler," in *Utah Historical Quarterly,* April, 1932, vol. V, pp-35-64; July, 1932, vol. V, pp. 87-112; October, 1932, vol. V, pp. 134-160.

Burdick, A.J. *The Mystic Mid-Region, the Deserts of the Southwest.* New York, Putnam, 1904.

Chalfant, W.A. *Death Valley: The Facts.* Stanford University, Stanford University Press, 1930, rev. ed., 1936.
Detailed accurate data on Death Valley.

Chalfant, W.A. *The Story of Inyo.* Chicago, 1922, rev. ed., Los Angeles Citizens Print Shop, Inc., 1933.

Chase, J.S. *California Desert Trails.* Boston, Houghton Mifflin, 1919.

Coolidge, Dane. *Death Valley Prospectors.* New York, E.P. Dutton and Co., Inc., 1937.
Personal experiences in Death Valley.

Coville, Dr. Frederick Vernon. *Botany of the Death Valley Expedition.* Washington, Government Printing Office, 1893; out of print.

Coville, Dr. Frederick Vernon. "The Panamint Indians of California," in *American Anthropologist,* October, 1892.

Evans, John Henry. *Charles Coulson Rich; Pioneer Builder of the West.* New York, Macmillan, 1936. 400 p. Illus.
Rich was one of the original settlers of San Bernardino, California, and crossed Death Valley in 1849.

Frémont, John Charles. *Memoirs of My Life.* Chicago, 1887.

Lee, Bourke. *Death Valley Men.* New York, Macmillan, 1932.
 The story of Death Valley Scotty and others in the Death Valley region, with descriptions of the trails.

Manly, William Lewis. *Death Valley in '49.* San Jose, the Pacific Tree and Vine Co., 1894; out of print. Rev. ed., New York, Wallace Hebbord, 1929.
 An account of a wagon train crossing of the plains by one of the party that named Death Valley.

Perkins, Edna Brush. *White Heart of Mojave, an Adventure with the Outdoors of the Desert.* New York, Horace Liveright, 1922; out of print.
 A story of two women, who, with a guide, two horses, and a wagon, camped in Death Valley and the high Panamints for several weeks.

Spears, John Randolph. *Illustrated Sketches of Death Valley and Other Borax Deserts of the Pacific Coast.* Chicago, Rand McNally & Co., 1892; out of print.

Wilson, Neill. *Silver Stampede.* New York; Macmillan, 1937.
 An account of Panamint City and two Nevada Senators.

Recommended Contemporary Reading

Lingenfelter, Richard E. *Death Valley & the Amargosa: A Land of Illusion.* University of California Press, Berkeley and Los Angeles, 1986.

O'Gara, Geoffrey. *A Long Road Home: In the Footsteps of the WPA Writers.* Boston, Houghton Mifflin Company, 1989.

Norwood, Vera and Janice Monk, eds. *The Desert is No Lady.* Yale University Press, New Haven and London, 1987.

Limerick, Patricia Nelson. *Desert Passages: Encounters with the American Deserts.* University of New Mexico Press, Albuquerque, 1985.

Wild, Peter, ed. *The Desert Reader.* University of Utah Press, Salt Lake City, 1991.

Zwinger, Ann Haymond. *The Mysterious Lands.* Truman Talley Books/ Plume, New York, 1989.

Groups of Interest

Death Valley Chamber of Commerce
#2 Post Office Row
Tecopa, CA 92389
(619) 852-4524

Death Valley '49ers
P.O. Box 339
Death Valley, CA 92328

Death Valley Natural History Association
P.O. Box 188
Death Valley, CA 92328

Friends of Rhyolite
P.O. Box 85
Amargosa Valley, NV 89020

Performance and Tour Information:

Amargosa Opera House
Post Office B
Death Valley Junction, CA 92328
(619) 852-4316

Index

159